LONGMAN

War

Major writers of the 19th and 20th centuries

Selected and edited by Jane Christopher

General editor: Michael Marland
Series consultant: Geoff Barton

LONGMAN

Longman Imprint Books
General editor: Michael Marland

New titles
Characters from Pre-20th-Century Novels
Diaries and Letters
Genres
Global Tales
Highlights from 19th-Century Novels
Landmarks
Mystery and Horror
Scenes from Plays
Starting Shakespeare
Stories from Africa
Stories from Europe
Stories Old and New
Ten Short Plays
Travel Writing
Two Centuries
War Stories

Previously published titles
Autobiographies selected and edited by Linda Marsh
Black Boy Richard Wright
Cider with Rosie Laurie Lee
The Diary of Anne Frank edited by Christopher Martin
Ghost Stories selected by Susan Hill
The Human Element and other stories Stan Barstow
I'm the King of the Castle Susan Hill
P'tang, Yang, Kipperbang and other TV plays Jack Rosenthal
A Roald Dahl Selection edited by Roy Blatchford
Stories from Asia selected and edited by Madhu Bhinda
Strange Meeting Susan Hill
The Woman in Black Susan Hill

Contents

The National Curriculum

The National Curriculum for English states that pupils should read selected short stories that: 'include a range of narrative structures and literary techniques; extend pupils' ideas and emotional understanding; offer perspectives on society and community and their impact on the lives of individuals'. It also recommends that pupils should read texts from other cultures and traditions that represent their 'distinctive voices and forms', and offer 'varied perspectives and subject matter'.

With this in mind, *War Stories* includes a selection of short stories written by women and men from different cultures. This variety provides interesting contrasts, not only in the individual's perspective of war but also in that of the culture in which they write. Students are also encouraged to compare the distinctive styles of each writer.

The activities for each story cover discussion work, language study and written assignments. The purpose is to encourage awareness of language, genre, social and historical context, and literary techniques. Coursework assignments are also included, making this a practical collection, through which pupils build their understanding by exploring the social and historical contexts of literature and by comparing texts.

Comparing the texts

While each story can be studied as an individual work of art, the collection is designed to help a variety of comparisons between stories. The sequence of the stories is printed in two broad groupings, making comparisons by background and theme: *During war and destruction* and *The consequences and effects of war*. Many other forms of comparison could also be made, and the following list shows alternative ways of making comparisons between the stories, providing the opportunity to focus on the comparisons in the social and historical context and in the literary voice.

Pre-twentieth-century comparisons

The Upturned Face and *Two Friends*

Twentieth-century comparisons

The Fly (third person) and *The Deserter* (first person)

First-person narrative comparisons

On the Quai at Smyrna, A Certain Death and *Summer Flower*

Third-person narrative comparisons

They Came, The Upturned Face and *The Alien Skull*

Wartime conditions

On the Quai at Smyrna, The Upturned Face and *Summer Flower*

Difficult decisions

A Certain Death and *Pigeons*

War glory

They Came and *The Deserter*

Attack from the outside

Summer Flower and *Two Friends*

War in two centuries

The Upturned Face and *The Making of Me*

A woman's perspective

A Certain Death and *The Fly*

Introduction

War seems to be a main ingredient of the news. Almost nightly, we see mounds of dead bodies, children with amputated limbs and soldiers lying in hospital with bandages covering their bullet holes. These images from reality are frequently upsetting, but what happens when we see too many, so many that we stop being upset and become almost indifferent?

Perhaps we should try a different perspective and think of the human price of war. After all, who thinks of the families that are related to each individual in that impersonal mound, or the future of the child with an amputated limb? The eyes that stare from the screen talk of many things: loss, confusion, anger and saturation. The child has also had enough. It could be that our failure to understand why the child has had to lose a limb at all and our feeling of helplessness cause this numbness.

In addition to reporting, television news and eyewitness accounts, war stories provide us with a different perspective. They allow us to see through the eyes of characters and, through the power of fiction, they can experiment with attitudes to war – using irony to create more subtle effects and using language creatively to capture the most appalling of human experiences.

The short stories contained in this anthology were written about different wars or destructive conflicts. The point here is that no matter the date, the country, or the number of people involved, all wars share main aspects in common: destruction, death, grief and hope. With this in mind, the stories have been arranged according to two broad groupings. The first is concerned with the period during war and destruction – how individuals and countries cope and what effect war has upon both. The second looks at the consequences and effects of war – how war can make individuals behave as a consequence and what results this can bring.

Some of these stories relate to specific incidents of war. For example, Tamiki Hara's story *Summer Flower* focuses upon the atomic bomb dropped on Hiroshima in August 1945, where more than seventy-eight thousand lives were lost. Hara witnessed the devastating effects of this bomb and tries to capture the feeling of chaos and grief in his story. What some stories also illustrate, however, is that it is possible to comment upon war while remaining outside it. An example of this is Katherine Mansfield's story *The Fly*, where we learn of the destructive effects of war upon those left behind. Mansfield lived through the First World War and her brother was killed in it. She used her experience to relate the anger of a man, deprived of his son, to the aggression he shows towards a defenceless fly. Both fact and fiction are used as vehicles for authors to express their opinions and attitudes towards war. You should consider carefully how a writer's experience has affected his or her writing and what he/she hoped to achieve in choosing that particular vehicle and voice.

The intention within each section of this anthology is to present aspects of war which you may not previously have considered, and to compare the way different writers present war as a human experience and the literary devices and approaches they use in their short stories. In doing this, we are pricking at the numbness, and paying respect not only to the many who have lost their lives but also to the living who want to live theirs.

Jane Christopher

On the Quai at Smyrna

by Ernest Hemingway

After the First World War, peace with Turkey proved difficult. The Sultan's government had accepted the peace terms of the Treaty of Sèvres in August 1920 but a Turkish general, Mustafa Kemal, led a revolt against the terms of peace. The Greeks landed troops in Turkish Asia Minor but were defeated by Kemal in September 1922. Kemal then turned his troops against the British, who were stationed in the Straits of Constantinople. Kemal achieved his aim of freeing Turkey from foreign invasions and, as a result, Turkey was proclaimed a republic and Kemal its first president. The story is set on the quay ('quai' is the French spelling) or wharf at Smyrna in western Turkey. It is now called Izmir and is a large seaport.

The strange thing was, he said, how they screamed every night at midnight. I do not know why they screamed at that time. We were in the harbour and they were all on the pier and at midnight they started screaming. We used to turn the searchlight on them to quiet them. That always did the trick. We'd run the searchlight up and down over them two or three times and they stopped it. One time I was senior officer on the pier and a Turkish officer[1] came up to me in a frightful rage because one of our sailors had been most insulting to him. So I told him the fellow would be sent on ship and be most severely punished. I asked him to

[1] officer in army led by Mustafa Kemal against the Greeks

point him out. So he pointed out a gunner's mate,[2] most inoffensive chap. Said he'd been most frightfully and repeatedly insulting; talking to me through an interpreter. I couldn't imagine how the gunner's mate knew enough Turkish to be insulting. I called him over and said, 'And just in case you should have spoken to any Turkish officers.'

'I haven't spoken to any of them, sir.'

'I'm quite sure of it,' I said, 'but you'd best go on board ship and not come ashore again for the rest of the day.'

Then I told the Turk the man was being sent on board ship and would be most severely dealt with. Oh most rigorously. He felt topping about it. Great friends we were.

The worst, he said, were the women with dead babies. You couldn't get the women to give up their dead babies. They'd have babies dead for six days. Wouldn't give them up. Nothing you could do about it. Had to take them away finally. Then there was an old lady, most extraordinary case. I told it to a doctor and he said I was lying. We were clearing them off the pier, had to clear off the dead ones, and this old woman was lying on a sort of litter. They said, 'Will you have a look at her, sir?' So I had a look at her and just then she died and went absolutely stiff. Her legs drew up and she drew up from the waist and went quite rigid. Exactly as though she had been dead over night. She was quite dead and absolutely rigid. I told a medical chap about it and he told me it was impossible.

They were all out there on the pier and it wasn't at all like an earthquake or that sort of thing because they never knew about the Turk. They never knew what the

[2] an aid to an artillery soldier

old Turk would do. You remember when they ordered us not to come in to take off any more? I had the wind up when we came in that morning. He had any amount of batteries[3] and could have blown us clean out of the water. We were going to come in, run close along the pier, let go the front and rear anchors and then shell the Turkish quarter of the town. They would have blown us out of water but we would have blown the town simply to hell. They just fired a few blank charges at us as we came in. Kemal came down and sacked the Turkish commander. For exceeding his authority or some such thing. He got a bit above himself. It would have been the hell of a mess.

You remember the harbour. There were plenty of nice things floating around in it. That was the only time in my life I got so I dreamed about things. You didn't mind the women who were having babies as you did those with the dead ones. They had them all right. Surprising how few of them died. You just covered them over with something and let them go to it. They'd always pick out the darkest place in the hold to have them. None of them minded anything once they got off the pier.

The Greeks were nice chaps too. When they evacuated they had all their baggage animals they couldn't take off with them so they just broke their forelegs and dumped them into the shallow water. All those mules with their forelegs broken pushed over into the shallow water. It was all a pleasant business. My word yes a most pleasant business.

[3] units of guns

A Certain Death

by Flora Nwapa

The Biafran War (1967–70) was a civil war in Nigeria. Two military coups in 1966 left Nigeria racked by ethnic divisions and on 26 May 1967 Lieutenant-Colonel Ojukwu declared the eastern region of Nigeria independent as the state of Biafra. Civil war then broke out as the federal government, led by General Gowon, sought to keep Nigeria together. It was not until January 1970 that peace was restored.

He was about eighteen years old, fair, very handsome and well built. I kept staring at him when he stood at attention and saluted me in military style. My mind was at rest. It was true what they had said of him.

The man had come to see us the previous day. I did not know him. I did not even know who had suggested to a friend that we should see him and that he would be able to help us.

This man was tough. It was not easy to place him. He was not an army officer. He did not look like a political thug nor a militia[1] in the then Biafra. He was plain tough.

He spoke to my brother who was unwell. I was there beside him. Only a month ago, he had lost his wife and two children in a gruesome air raid that struck in the market place. The wife was returning from the market, when the jets descended. She had no time to take cover.

[1] military force

It appeared as if they had come purposely for her. In an instant, she was struck, and her head was severed from her body. Then the rest of the body convulsed in death throes,[2] jerked a few yards, and died, a second time.

At that very moment, the two children playing in front of the house were killed in the same raid.

The people marvelled. 'The couple must be evil. Air raid, like thunder, doesn't strike innocent people. They must be guilty of some crime. A mother and her two children to die in one air raid! It is most unnatural.'

My brother went off his head. He was still dazed as the remnants of flesh that were once his wife's and children's were gathered and put in one hurriedly made coffin.

'Throw them away, why bother to make a coffin,' some people had whispered. But I insisted that at least a coffin should be provided for the pieces of human flesh.

My mind went back to the first air raid in Port Harcourt.[3] A prominent businessman had been struck as he was descending the steps of his storey building. The contents of his brief case had been revealed in which there was some deal with the Federal Military Government. And besides he was an evil and heartless businessman who did not hesitate to fight his business competitors with any available weapon. It was right and just that he should meet his death in the way he did.

I had believed everything I heard about the man. And perhaps, if I were in Port Harcourt, I would have joined the crowd that went to see the pieces of flesh of a saboteur.

For days my brother was dazed. He could say nothing

[2] struggling in anguish
[3] seaport in the then Biafra

and he could eat nothing. I was beside him. I was then the only possession he had. I was his only sister. We had no brother. Our parents had died when we were young.

'Leave my brother alone,' I said to the man. 'I sent for you. Tell me what you want, and I'll give it to you. You see him there, he has nobody but me. I have nothing, but him. I'll sell myself to see that he does not go to war. So what do you want?'

'Young woman, please don't be so snappy. I want to help you. I have helped many like you. I am not a mercenary.[4] You have a genuine case. They can shoot me if they know what I am trying to do. The youth I am going to bring to you tomorrow has been employed before by many people. This is not the first time nor the second. His father knows all about it. In fact the money we ask for would be sent to his father. His father is in great hardship. His children are starving. This is all the youth can do to help him and his young sisters and brothers.'

'You are most kind. I understand. Please pardon me. How much then?'

'Only four hundred pounds, and one hundred for me, and fifty for the youth to bribe his way through.'

I counted the money and gave it to him. He counted it very carefully. 'Keep fifty pounds,' he said. 'When I bring him in the morning, you give it to him. Four hundred pounds I'll give his father before he releases him to me.'

I was not engaged in the attack trade. I bought and sold in the local market while I waited for the war to end. I had sold two eight pieces of 'jorge' for five hundred pounds for this purpose. I did not want to borrow. Nobody would of course lend me money without asking questions.

[4] working merely for money

What did I not do to save my brother from this certain death? Conscription[5] was certain death for him. The people had demanded that he should go to war before he brought ruin to the town. Someone who lost a wife and two children in one day must be evil. He must have done something to merit the punishment. If he was not got rid of, the whole town would suffer.

I was trading in Lagos[6] when the crisis started. I was the first among the other women trading in Balogun Street to return. My husband was working in one of the Ministries in Lagos. He was attending a course in the USA when the coup[7] took place. He sent a frantic cable[8] to me asking me to take our three children home immediately. I obeyed.

I hired a vehicle from a relation of my husband's, put my three children in the vehicle, and begged him to take them home, while I collected debts from my numerous debtors.

My children, the driver and my personal belongings never reached my home. There was an accident near Ore and all the passengers were killed. My husband preferred to remain in the USA after this tragedy.

Was there any wonder that our people were afraid that my brother and I could bring them further disaster? If they got rid of my brother by sending him to this certain death, they would avert the disaster. So I was bent on seeing that he was not sacrificed, even if it meant my own death.

So that morning, the youth was in front of me. 'Please sit down,' I said. He refused to sit down. The

[5] compulsory military service
[6] capital of Nigeria
[7] violent or illegal change of government
[8] message sent by telegraph wires

tough man had left. I could not help noticing that he left in a hurry and that there was pain in his eyes.

My brother came out this time and sat down in the only available chair. He was still unwell, and there was evidence that he had cried in the night. 'Did you hear them this morning?' he asked me. I nodded.

'Never mind,' I said. 'Nothing will happen to you. As long as I am alive nothing will ever happen to you.'

I hadn't told him what I intended doing. He saw the youth, but he had not the slightest idea of what he was doing in the house. I'll tell him, not now, later. If I told him then, he would ask questions and I was not prepared to give answers to the questions. I was bent on saving his life. Was I bent on killing the youth?

My blood ran cold. Kill the youth. Of course he was not going to die. I was assured. He had done it twice. The third time might be tough, might even cost him his life. God forbid! He will come back. He will surely come back. My God, what was happening to me? to us? to the whole world?

I got up. I called the maid. 'Agnes, please give him food to eat. I have everything prepared. I'll soon be back.'

What if he escaped when I was away? I had spent five hundred pounds already. I had nothing else left to sell except my bed. Perhaps I'd sell that too if he escaped. No, he will not escape. The tough man had reassured me. My brother did not ask me where I was going.

I knocked at the door of the man in charge of conscription. The door was opened and I walked in. He offered me a seat. I sat down and looked intently at him. He pretended not to know why I had come. The silence was getting longer, so he began: 'Just tell me why your brother should not fight for the liberation of Biafra?'

Instantly, I wanted to reply: 'And you, could you tell me why you yourself are in charge of conscription and not my brother?'

I restrained myself. There was absolutely no reason why I should be offensive. We were at war with the whole world. We were in a state of emergency. Unimportant people had overnight become Very Important People. If one played one's card very well, one would survive. I was not going to cause the death of my brother by being stupid. I had to be diplomatic.[9]

'He is my only brother. He is all I have in the world. He has never killed a fly. Please help me. Do all you can for me. God will reward you. Everyone knows my story. Save my brother; you never know, this war will end, my brother may be of help to you in normal times. You know about my husband. They say he is dead, I don't think so. He is in America. He is quite high in government. You never can tell, he might be of use too. Please have pity.'

He smiled. 'My two children are in the army. We are at war with Nigeria. They killed us like flies in the north. We must fight for our freedom. There is no going back. It has come to the stage when all of us should be called. He must go. When I am called I too must go. Those Biafran youths dying were born of women. They were human beings like you and I. So I don't see why your brother should not go to war.'

He got up and said he was attending a meeting, and that he was in fact late already. I too got up. I was thinking fast. What was I going to do next? 'Where do I go?' I asked him.

'Go home,' he said irritably. I smiled.

'I am going home.'

[9] tactful

He smiled in spite of himself. Then he said, not really to me but to himself, 'Ike Ugo must be asked to explain certain things about this conscription. He seems to be lukewarm about a number of things. However . . .'

'Who is Ike Ugo?' I asked myself as I went home with a heavy heart. 'I have heard of him. In what connection? In what connection? In what . . .'

Of course I knew Ike Ugo. In the good old days his sister and I were great friends. We both married, got busy in our homes and saw little of each other. I was not sure whether Ike would remember me. If his sister had returned as I did, it would have been easy, but she did not return. I must go to him, perhaps he had something to do with this conscription, otherwise the man in charge of conscription would not have mentioned his name. I could see that he was not pleased with the way Ike Ugo was handling things. Perhaps Ike was more humane about it all.

Ike was in. Fortunately, he remembered me. I asked about his sister and family. They were in Lagos, he said. Somehow, he went on, he managed to hear from them. He had heard about me and my woes, and he was very sorry. Then he said, 'What can I do for you, my sister's friend?'

Before I said anything, I wiped the tears from my eyes, then carefully, I told him the plight[10] that I was in.

'You should not have gone to him,' he said. 'I am in charge of it all. Have you someone to go in place of your brother?'

'Yes,' I said.

'Can you bring him tomorrow to me in the office?'

'He is in my house right now,' I said.

'You have no problem. I shall come and collect him

[10] difficult situation

when we finish the meeting. There is no problem at all. The youth would not even answer your brother's name. He would answer his own name. I shall tick your brother's name as having fulfilled all the conditions. Never mind. There is no problem.' At this juncture he enumerated the names of the people who had already passed through this ordeal. And added. 'Ask your brother to be scarce for at least three weeks.'

It was too good to be true. I got up. 'Ike,' I said. 'How do I thank you?' He only smiled.

'Don't worry. We shall all survive.'

I went home. The youth was there. He stood at attention again and saluted. Why is he so respectful? I wanted to ask him to confirm what I had heard of him, namely, that it was his will and that of his father that he should employ himself in this way. That he knew his way about and had in fact gone to fight in place of two people in the past. But I had no courage to ask him. He was too handsome, too young to employ himself in that dangerous way. And besides I wanted at all costs to save the life of my only brother.

I asked Agnes whether he had eaten. 'Yes, he has eaten,' she said and smiled. 'He ate up everything and asked, shyly, for more.'

'And did you give him?'

'No, I didn't. That was all I had for him.'

I wanted to call Agnes all sorts of names I could think of, but restrained myself. I went to the kitchen and prepared something quickly for the youth. He was grateful. He ate up everything again.

At this time, my brother was out and I waited for Ike to come. I prayed that he should come before my brother returned from wherever he went. I wanted to spare him the agony of any further transaction that might ensue again. He knew I was up to something. But he did not want to discuss it. He was really not interested in anything.

'I lost my wife and children the same day. What else matters? If they want me to go to war, I'll go. It is the easiest way to die these days. Nobody would accuse you of suicide.'

Suicide it was. To be compelled to go to war and to be conscripted into the Biafran army was suicide, pure and simple. Only those who possessed the 'sixth sense' survived. Like the youth who was now going to take the place of my brother. I had bought him to 'die' in place, not of, but for my brother. Nobody was prepared to die for anybody. But why should anyone want to die for another? It did not make sense at all. Death was no joke. If you died, you died, and that was the end of you.

'We shall all survive.' The words of Ike kept ringing in my ears. Perhaps we shall all survive. Who knows? Perhaps we should all die before the war ended. Who knows? Only God knew. God, please be merciful to us and save us from death, from air raids, from accidental discharges, from night-marauders,[11] from deserters, from saboteurs, from white mercenaries, from over-zealous leaders.

I waited for Ike for nearly an hour, but he did not come. An unknown fear gripped me. Why hadn't he come? He said he would come and take the youth immediately. No, he said he would attend a meeting first. Which meeting was that? There were so many meetings in those days. People simply loved meetings. One did not only go to a meeting to air one's views; one went to listen and to be listened to. One wanted to score points. To bring it to the knowledge of everyone that one knew how to talk, that one was very important.

[11] those who make raids at night

The youth was there. He was so relaxed and this comforted me. It made me relax as well for a little while. I waited for Ike. He will come. He was such a nice person. He was not going to let me down.

Then I heard a conversation. It was coming nearer and nearer. 'What he was saying,' said one, 'was that nobody was too big to go to war. That he had sacrificed two of his sons and so everybody should sacrifice his sons as well.'

'No, that was not what he meant exactly. What he meant was that he had already sacrificed two boys in the war, and everybody should do the same. Everybody who had sons to sacrifice. I have no male child, thank God.'

'Childless mothers seem to be quite happy at this conscription you know.'

'Why not? Conscription is certain death. The quickest way to die. Those conscripted have no training at all. Didn't you know?'

Did the youth hear? Perhaps he heard. Was he still willing to go? What if he melted away before Ike came? I had paid for him to replace my brother. If he disappeared without fulfilling the contract there was nothing I could do. Nothing. Absolutely nothing. God have mercy on us.

At last Ike came. He was in a hurry. 'Where is he?' he asked.

I took him to where the boy was. 'Let's go then, they are waiting for us.'

The youth got up, and obeyed. I pressed fifty pounds into his palm. He gripped the money. He did not turn back. I watched him go with Ike. Why should people go to war? Why should people resort to force? I was sending this boy, who was old enough to be my son to a certain death. No, I was not. He was not going to fight. He said he had gone twice. This was his third time. He said he was well known in Orlu and therefore would not want to go there. He was going to Owerri.[12] He was not known in Owerri. He knew his way about. I should not worry.

But I worried as Ike took him. I had seen those conscripted before. They looked wretched. There was one particular one who wept all through. He did not return. His aged mother is still waiting for him. He will never return.

About a week later, early in the morning, the crier piped out: 'The village of Amosu, the village of Amosu. Do you hear? Open your ears and hear me. You are in arrears of men for the army. Do you hear, you are in arrears of men. This is the last warning. On Afo day, you must present the men for the army. If you don't your village head will be handed over to the army. Don't say you were not warned. You are the only village in arrears.'

I shivered. The youth had replaced my brother, thank God. My brother had left the town. Nobody would see him until this cruel war was over.

[12] town north of Port Harcourt

They Came

by Alun Lewis

The evening was slowly curdling[1] the sky as the soldier trudged the last mile along the lane leading from the station to the Hampshire village where he was billeted.[2] The hedgerows drew together in the dusk and the distance, bending their waving heads to each other as the fawn bird and the blackbird sang among the green hollies. The village lay merged in the soft seaward slope of the South Downs; the soldier shifted his rifle from left to right shoulder and rubbed his matted eyelashes with his knuckles. He was a young chap but, hampered by his heavy greatcoat and equipment, he dragged his legs like an old clerk going home late. He cleared his throat of all that the train journey, cigarettes and chocolate and tea and waiting had secreted in his mouth. He spat the thick saliva out. It hung on a twig.

Someone was following him. When he heard the footsteps first he had hurried, annoyed by the interfering sound. But his kit was too clumsy to hurry in and he was too tired. So he dawdled, giving his pursuer a chance to pass him. But the footsteps stayed behind, keeping a mocking interval. He couldn't stop himself listening to them, but he refused to look back. He became slowly angry with himself for letting them occupy his mind and possess his attention. After a while

[1] turning from a liquid to a semi-solid mass; usually associated with milk
[2] a billet is a non-military place where a soldier is lodged

they seemed to come trotting out of the past in him, out of the Welsh mining village, the colliers gambling in the quarry, the county school where he learned of sex and of knowledge, and college where he had swotted and slacked in poverty, and boozed, and quarrelled in love. They were the footsteps of the heavy-jawed deacon of Zion,[3] with his white grocer's apron, and his hairy nostrils sniffing out corruption.

But that was silly, he knew. Too tired to control his mind, that's what it was. These footsteps were natural and English, the postman's perhaps ... But still they followed him, and the dark gods wrestling in him in the mining valley pricked their goaty ears at the sound of the pimping[4] feet.

He turned the corner into the village and went down the narrow street past the post office and the smithy, turned the corner under the AA sign and crossed the cobbled yard of the hotel where the officers' and business men's cars were parked. A shaggy old dog came frisking out of its straw-filled barrel in the corner, jumping and barking. He spoke to it and at once it grovelled on its belly. He always played with the dog in the mornings, between parades. The unit did its squad drill in the hotel yard, kitchen maids watching flirtatiously through the windows, giggling, and the lavatory smelling either of disinfectant or urine.

He pushed open the little door in the big sliding doors of the garage which had been converted into a barrack room for the duration. The electric bulbs high in the cold roof dangled a weak light from the end of the twisted, wavering flex. Grey blankets folded over biscuits or straw palliasses[5] down both sides of the

[3] a minister in the Christian Church (Zion is a name for Jerusalem)
[4] possibly meaning small, mean or sickly
[5] mattresses

room. Equipment hanging from nails on the white-washed wall – in one corner a crucifix, over the thin, chaste, taciturn Irish boy's bed. He was the only one in the room, sitting on his bed in the cold dark corner writing in his diary. He looked up and smiled politely, self-effacingly, said, 'Hallo. Had a good leave?' and bent his narrow head again to read what he had written.

'Yes, thanks,' said the soldier, 'except for raids. The first night I was home he raided us for three hours, the sod,' he said, unbuckling his bayonet belt and slipping his whole kit off his shoulders.

Last time he returned from leave, four months back, he had sat down on his bed and written to his wife. They had married on the first day of that leave and slept together for six nights. This time he didn't ferret in his kitbag for notepaper and pencil. He went straight out.

The hotel management had set a room aside for the soldiers to booze in. It was a good class hotel, richly and vulgarly finished with plush mirrors and dwarf palms in green boxes. The auctioneers and lawyers and city men, the fishermen and golfers and bank managers, most of whom had weekend cottages or villas of retirement in commanding positions at the local beauty spots, spent the evening in the saloon bar and lounge, soaking and joking. So the soldiers were given a bare little bar parlour at the back, with a fire and a dartboard and two sawdust spittoons.[6] The soldiers were glad of it. It was their own. They invited some of their pals from the village to play darts with them – the cobbler, the old dad who lived by himself in the church cottage and never shaved or washed, the poacher who brought them a plucked pheasant under his old coat

[6] bowls to spit into

sometimes – all the ones the soldiers liked popped in for an evening. A few girls, too, before the dance in the church hall, on Tuesdays.

Fred Garstang from Portsmouth and Ben Bryant from Coventry, the two oldest soldiers in the unit – regulars who had never carried a stripe – were playing darts, two empty pint glasses on the mantelpiece by the chalk and duster.

'Owdee, Taffy?' they said in unison. ''Ave a good leave, lad?'

'Yes, thanks,' he said automatically, 'except for raids. The sod raided us for three hours the first night I was home.'

'Damn. Just the wrong side of it,' said Fred, examining the quivering dart. 'I deserve to lose this bloody game, Ben. I 'xpect you're same as me, Taff; glad to get back to a bit of peace and quiet and a good sleep. My seven days in Pompey's[7] the worst I've ever spent in India, China, the Rhineland, Gallygurchy, or anywhere. But we're nice and cosy here, thank God. They can keep their leave. *I* don't want seven nights in an Anderson.[8] I'd rather stay here, I would.'

Old Fred never stopped talking once he started. The soldier tapped the counter with a shilling and leaned over to see whether the barmaid was on the other side of the partition. He saw her silky legs and the flutter of her skirt. He hit the counter harder, then, while he waited, wondered at his impatience. His body wasn't thirsty; it was too damned tired to bother, too worn-out. It was something else in him that wanted to get drunk, dead, dead drunk.

The barmaid came along, smiling. She was natural

[7] slang for Portsmouth
[8] small air-raid shelter for a family, built in the garden

with the soldiers. She smiled when she saw who it was and held her pretty clenched fist to him across the counter. He should have taken it and forced it gently open, of course. Instead, he just put his flat palm underneath it. She looked at him with a hurt-fawn reproach in her smiling eyes, and opening her hand let a toffee fall into his.

'One from the wood, Madge,' he said.

'I'll have to charge you for *that,* ' she said.

'That's all right,' he replied. 'You always pay in this life.'

'Why don't you take the girl, Taffy?' said old Fred as he came and sat by them, their darts over. 'If I was your age . . .'

He had been in the army since he was fifteen. Now he was past soldiering, wandering in the head sometimes, doing odd jobs; in peace time he kept the lawns trimmed at the depot, now he was tin-man in the cooking-shed, cleaning with Vim the pots and pans Ben Bryant used for cooking. 'Vermicelli tastes all right,' he said. 'Better than anything you can pick up in the streets. Yellow or black, or white, German or Irish. I've never had a Russian though, never. It's not bad when you're young, like a new crane when the jib[9] runs out nice and smooth; it's better than sitting in the trenches like an old monkey, scratching yourself and not knowing whose leg it is or whose arm it is, looking in his pockets to see if there's anything worth taking, and not knowing who'll win the race, the bullet with your number on it or the leaky rod you're nursing. But I like it here. It's nice and peaceful up here, in the cookhouse all day. We ought to try some vermicelli, Ben, one day.'

'Don't you get impatient now, Freddy,' Ben said with

[9] protecting arm of a crane

the calmness of a father of many children. 'We'll stuff your pillow full of it next Christmas and put a sprig of it on your chest. Don't you worry, boy.'

But old Fred went on talking like an old prophet in a volcanic world, about and about. 'There's no knowing when you've got to fight for your king and country,' he said. 'No matter who you are, Russian, or Frenchy, or Jerry – and the Yankee, too. He'll be in it, boy. I've seen him die. It's only natural, to my way of thinking. I wore a pair of gloves the Queen knitted herself, she did, last time. The Unknown Soldier I was, last time.'

None of us are ourselves now, the Welsh boy sat thinking: neither what we were, nor what we will be. He drained his pint glass and crossed to the counter, to Madge smiling there.

'You never looked round all the way up from the station,' she said, pulling her shoulder-straps up under her grey jumper and exposing the white rich flesh above her breasts.

'So it was you followed me, eh?' he said sardonically.

'Why didn't you turn round?' she asked. 'Did you know it was me? You knew someone was behind you, I could tell.'

'I didn't turn round because I didn't want to look *back*,' he said.

'And you mean to say you don't know how the Hebrew puts out the eyes of a goldfinch?' Freddy's aggrieved voice swirled up.

'Afraid of being homesick for your wife, eh?' she jeered.

He covered his eyes with his hand, tired out, and looked up at the vague sensual woman playing upon his instincts there like a gipsy on a zither.

'Not homesick,' he said drily. 'Deathsick.'

'What d'you mean?' she said.

'Well, she was killed in a raid,' he shouted.

He went up to the orderly room then, having forgotten to hand in his leave pass to the orderly corporal. The room was in the corner of an old warehouse. The building also housed the kitchen and the quartermaster's stores. About the high bare rooms with their rotten dry floors and musty walls, rats galloped in the darkness; in the morning their dirt lay fresh on the mildewed sacks and the unit's cat stretched her white paws and got a weak and lazy thrill from sniffing it.

The orderly corporal was dozing over a Western novelette from Woolworth's, hunched up in a pool of lamp- and firelight.

'Hallo, Taffy,' he said. 'Had a good leave?'

'Yes, thanks,' he replied. 'Except for raids. Am I on duty tomorrow?'

'You're on duty tonight, I'm afraid,' the orderly corporal replied with the unctuous mock-regret of one who enjoys detailing tired or refractory men for unexpected jobs.

'Dave Finley had a cold on his chest this morning and didn't get out of bed. So they fetched him out on a stretcher and the MO gave him pneumonia pills before Dave could stop him; so he's got pneumonia now. You'll go on guard at midnight and at six hours.'

'OK.'

He turned to go.

'Better get some sleep,' said the orderly corporal, yawning noisily. 'Hell! I'm browned off with this war.'

The soldier yawned too, and laughed, and returned to the barrack-room to lie down for a couple of hours. He rolled his blankets down on the floor and stretched out.

Old Ben and Fred were back, also, Ben fixing

bachelor buttons into his best trousers and singing Nelly Dean comfortably to himself, Fred muttering by the stove. 'There's some mean and hungry lads in this room,' he said; 'very hungry and mean. It's an awful nature, that. They'll borrow off you all right, but they won't lend you the turd off their soles. And always swanking in the mirror, and talking all the time, saying, yes, they can do the job easy. The fools! Whip 'em! Whip 'em!'

Ben was toasting bread on the point of his bayonet and boiling water in his billy.[10] A tin of pilchards left over from tea was for them all.

'Come on, Taffy. Have a bellyful while you can,' he said.

'No, thanks,' said the soldier, restless on his blankets. 'I don't feel like food tonight, Ben, thanks.'

'Ain't you never bin hungry?' Fred shouted, angrily. 'You don't know what food is, you youngsters don't.'

'I've been without food,' the soldier said, thinking of the '26 strike;[11] and going without peas and chips in the chip shop by the town clock in college, when a new book must be bought. But not now, when everything is free but freedom, and the doctor and dentist and cobbler send you no bills. What survives I don't know, the soldier thought, rubbing his hot eyelids and shifting his legs on the spreadout blankets. What is it that survives?

He got up and buckled his battle order together, adjusting his straps, slipping the pull-through through his Enfield,[12] polishing boots and buttons, tightening his helmet strap under his chin.

[10] metal can for cooking, usually on a camp fire
[11] referring to the General Strike of 4–12 May 1926 organised by the Trades Union Congress in support of an existing miners' strike to resist wage cuts
[12] a type of rifle

'There was a religious woman used to come to our house,' Ben was saying, 'and one day she said to me, sociable like, "You're a Guinness drinker, aren't you, Mr Bryant?" and I says, "I am, mum." And she says, "Well, can you tell me what's wrong with the ostrich on them advertisements?"'

The soldier went out to relieve the guard.

They were only twenty soldiers altogether, sent up here to guard a transmitting station hidden in the slopes of the Downs. A cushy job, safe as houses. There was a little stone shed, once used for sheep that were sick after lambing, in a chalky hollow on the forehead of the hill, which the guard used for sleeping in when they were off duty. Two hours on, four hours off, rain and sun and snow and stars. As the soldier toiled up the lane and across the high meadows to the shed, the milky moon came out from grey clouds and touched with lucid fingers the chopped branches piled in precise lengths at the foot of the wood. The pine trees moved softly as the moon touched their grey-green leaves, giving them a veil that looked like rainy snow, grey-white.

The lane running up through the wood shortened alarmingly in perspective. A star fell. So surprising, so swift and delicate, the sudden short curved fall and extinction of the tiny lit world. But over it the Plough still stayed, like something imperishable in man. He leant against the gate, dizzy and light-headed, waves of soft heat running into his head. He swallowed something warm and thick; spitting it out, he saw it was blood. He stayed there a little, resting, and then went on.

He went along the sandy lane, noticing as he always did the antique sculptures of sea and ice and rain, the smooth twisted flints, yellow and blue and mottled, lying in the white sand down which the water of winter scooped its way.

At the top of the lane was the lambing shed – guard room. He slipped quickly through the door to prevent any light escaping. There was gunfire and the sound of bombs along the coast.

The sergeant of the guard was lying on a palliasse in front of the stove. He got up slowly, groaning lazily. 'So you're back again, Taffy, are you?' he said, a grudge in his too hearty welcome. 'Relieving Dave Finley, eh? He's swinging the lead,[13] Dave is. I've a good mind to report him to the OC. It's tough on you, going on night guard after a day's journey. Have a good leave, Taff?'

'Not bad,' the soldier replied, 'except for the raids. Raided us the first night I was home.'

'It's a sod, everybody's getting it,' the sergeant replied, yawning. 'They dropped two dozen incendiaries in our fields in Lincs last week.'

He was drinking a billy can of cocoa which he had boiled on the fire, but he didn't offer any. He had weak blue eyes, a receding chin, fresh features of characterless good-looks, wavy hair carefully combed and brilliantined. He was always on edge against Taffy, distrusting him, perhaps envying him. He lived in terror of losing a stripe and in constant hunger to gain another promotion. He sucked and scraped the officers for this, zealously carrying out their orders with the finicky short temper of a weak house-proud woman. He polished the barrack-room floor and black-leaded the stove himself because the boys refused to do more than give the place a regulation lick. And he leaped at the chance of putting a man on the peg, he was always waiting to catch somebody cutting a church parade or

[13] pretending to be ill

nipping out of camp to meet a girl when he should be on duty. Yet he was mortally afraid of a quarrel, of unpopularity, and he was always jovial, glassily jovial, even to the Welsh boy whom he knew he couldn't deceive.

'Who am I to relieve on guard?' the soldier asked.

'Nobby Sherraton. He's patrolling the ridge.'

'OK.' He slipped his rifle sling over his shoulder and put his helmet on. 'You marching me out? Or shall I just go and send Nobby in?'

For once laziness overcame discretion.

'There's nobody about. Just go yourself,' the sergeant said, smiling, posing now as the informal honest soldier. 'I'll be seeing yer.'

'Some day.'

He left the hut and crossed the dry dead-white grass to the ridge where Nobby was on guard.

Nobby was his mate.

He had only been in the unit about a month. Before that he had been stationed just outside London and had done a lot of demolition and rescue work. He was from Mile End, and had roughed it. His hands and face showed that, his rough blackened hands, cigarette-stained, his red blotchy face with the bulbous nose, and the good blue eyes under tiny lids, and short scraggy lashes and brows. His hair was mousy and thin. He had been on the dole most of the time. He had been an unsuccessful boxer; he cleared out of that game when his brother, also a boxer, became punch-drunk and blind. He had plenty of tales of the Mosley faction.[14] He was sometimes paid five bob to break up their meetings. He always took his five bob, but he let the others do the

[14] Oswald Mosley was the leader of a Fascist party in the 1930s; meetings were often violent

breaking up. Who wants a black eye and a cut face for five bob? 'Tain't worth it. He rarely said anything about women. He didn't think much of lots of them; though like all Cockney youths he loved the 'old lady', his mother. He wasn't married. No, sir.

He was a conscript. Naturally. He didn't believe in volunteering. And he didn't like the Army, its drills and orders and its insistence on a smart appearance. Smartness he disliked. Appearances he distrusted. Orders he resented. He was 'wise' to things. No sucker.

Taffy felt a warm little feeling under his skin, relief more than anything else, to see Nobby again. He hadn't to pretend with Nobby. Fundamentally they shared the same humanity, the unspoken humanity of comradeship, of living together, sharing what they had, not afraid to borrow or talk or shut up. Or to leave each other and stroll off to satisfy the need for loneliness.

Nobby was surprised so much that he flung out his delight in a shout and a laugh and a wave of his arms.

'Taffy, lad!' he said. 'Back already, eh? Boy!' Then he became normal.

'Can't keep away from this bloody sannytorium[15] for long, can we?' he grumbled.

Taffy stood looking at him, then at the ground, then he turned away and looked nowhere.

'What's wrong, kid?' Nobby said, his voice urgent and frightened, guessing. 'Anything bad? Caught a packet, did you?' He said the last two phrases slowly, his voice afraid to ask.

'*I* didn't,' Taffy said, his voice thin and unsteady, '*I* didn't. *I'm* all right. *I'm* healthy.'

Nobby put his hand on his shoulder and turned him

[15] sanatorium – institute for invalids

round. He looked at the white sucked-in face and the eyes looking nowhere.

'Did *she* get it?' and he too turned his head a little and swallowed. 'She did,' he said, neither asking a question nor making a statement. Something absolute, the two words he said.

Taffy sat down, stretched out. The grass was dead; white, wispy long grass; Nobby sat down, too.

'They came over about eight o'clock the first night,' Taffy said. 'The town hadn't had a real one before. I've told you we've only got apartments, the top rooms in an old couple's house. The old ones got hysterics, see, Nobby. And then they wouldn't do what I told them, get down the road to a shelter. They wouldn't go out into the street and they wouldn't stay where they were. "My chickens," the old man was bluttering all the time. He's got an allotment up on the voel,[16] see. Gwyneth made them some tea. She was fine, she calmed them down. That was at the beginning, before the heavy stuff began. I went out the back to tackle the incendiaries. The boy next door was out there, too. He had a shovel and I fetched a saucepan. But it was freezing, and we couldn't dig the earth up quick enough. There were too many incendiaries. One fell on the roof and stuck in the troughing. The kid shinned up the pipe. It exploded in his face and he fell down. Twenty-odd feet. I picked him up and both his eyes were out, see?'

He had gone back to the sing-song rhythm and the broad accent of his home, the back lanes and the back gardens. He was shuddering a little, and sick-white, sallow. Nobby waited.

'I took him into his own house,' he said, controlling his voice now, almost reflective. 'I left him to his sister,

[16] hill or mountain

poor kid. Then I went in to see if Gwyneth was all right. She was going to take the old couple down the road to the shelter. She had a mack on over her dressing gown. We'd intended going to bed early, see? So I said she was to stay in the shelter. But she wanted to come back. We could lie under the bed together.

'I wanted her back, too, somehow. Then some more incendiaries fell, so I said, "Do as you like," and went at them with a saucepan. I thought sure one would blow my eyes out. Well, she took them down. Carried their cat for them. Soon as she'd gone the heavy stuff came. Oh, Christ!'

Nobby let him go on; better let him go on.

'It knocked me flat, dazed me for a bit. Then I got up and another one flattened me. It was trying to stop me, see, Nobby. I crawled out of the garden, but it was dark as hell, and buildings all down, dust and piles of masonry. Then he dropped some more incendiaries and the fires started. I knew she must be somewhere, see? I knew she must be somewhere. I began pulling the masonry away with my hands, climbed on to the pile of it in the fire. I couldn't see with the smoke and I knew it wasn't any use, only I had to do it, see?

'Then suddenly the masonry fell downwards. The road was clear on the other side. I thought it was all right after all, then. I thought she'd have reached the shelter ... But she hadn't ... I found her about twenty yards down the road ...

'She wasn't dead. Her clothes were gone. And her hands. She put them over her face, I reckon.

'She couldn't speak, but I know she knew it was me. I carried her back in my arms. Over the fallen house. The fire wasn't bad by then. Took her home, see, Nobby. Only the home was on fire. I wanted her to die all the time. I carried her over a mile through the streets. Fires and hoses and water. And she wouldn't die. When I got her to the clearing station I began to think she'd live. But they were only playing a game with me, see?'

He stood up, and made himself calm.

'Well, there it is.' He rubbed his face with the palm of his hand, wiping the cold sweat off.

'I knew she was going to die. When they told me she was – I didn't feel anything, Nobby ... But she died while they were messing her body about with their hands, see? ... And she never said anything. Never said anything to me. Not that it makes any difference, I suppose. We never did speak about those things much. Only, you know how it is, you want a word somehow. You want it to keep.'

'Sure, I know,' Nobby said.

'What's it all for, Nobby?' he said in a while. He looked so tired and beat. 'I used to know what it was all about, but I can't understand it now.'

'Aw, forget all about that,' Nobby said. 'You're here, aincher, now?'

He put his hands on his mate's shoulders and let him lean against him for a bit. 'I reckon you belong to each other for keeps, now,' Nobby said.

'You believe that, Nobby?' he asked, slow and puzzled, but with a gathering force as his uncertainty came together.

'Yes. For you and 'er, I do. It wouldn't be true for me, or the sergeant in there, but for you two it is.'

Taffy was still against his shoulder. Then slowly he straightened himself, moved back on to himself, and lifting his face he looked at the milky-white fields and the sentinel pines and the stars.

'I knew it was so, really,' he said. 'Only I was afraid I was fooling myself.'

He smiled, and moved his feet, pressing on them with his whole weight as if testing them after an illness.

'I'm all right, now, Nobby. Thank you, boy.'

'I'll go, then,' Nobby said. He slipped his rifle over his shoulder and as he moved off he hesitated, turned back, and touched his mate's arm lightly.

'Two's company, three's none,' he said, and stumped off slowly to the lambing shed through the dead straw-grass.

And the soldier was left alone on the flat upland ridge.

Below him the valleys widened into rich arable lakes on which the moonlight and the mist lay like the skeins which spiders spin round their eggs. Beyond the pools another chain of downland lay across the valleys, and beyond those hills the coast. Over him, over the valleys, over the pinewoods, blue fingers came out of the earth and moved slanting across their quarters as the bombers droned in the stars over his head and swung round to attack the coastal city from inland. The sky over the coast was inflamed and violent, a soft blood-red.

The soldier was thinking of the day he received his calling up papers, just a year ago. Sitting on the dry stone wall of his father's back garden with Gwyneth by him; his ragged little brother kneeling by the chicken-run, stuffing cabbage stumps through the netting for the hens to peck, and laughing and pulling the stumps out as the old hen made an angry jab; his father riddling the ashes and the ramshackle garden falling to bits, broken trellis and tottering fence; his mother washing her husband's flannel vest and drawers in the tub, white and vexed. He had taken Gwyneth's hand, and her hand had said, 'In coming and in going you are mine; now, and for a little while longer; and then for ever.'

But it was not her footsteps that followed him down the lane from the station.

Now over his head the darkness was in full leaf, drifted with the purity of pines, the calm and infinite darkness of an English night, with the stars moving in slow declension down the sky. And the warm scent of resin about him and of birds and of all small creatures moving in the loose mould in the ferns like fingers in velvet.

And the soldier stood under the pines, watching the night move down the valleys and lift itself seawards, hearing the sheep cough and farm dogs restlessly barking in the farms. And farther still the violence growing in the sky till the coast was a turbulent thunder of fire and sickening explosions, and there was no darkness there at all, no sleep.

'My life belongs to the world,' he said. ' I will do what I can.'

He moved along the spur and looked down at the snow-grey evergreen woods and the glinting roofs scattered over the rich land.

And down in the valleys the church bells began pealing, pealing, and he laughed like a lover, seeing his beloved.

The Upturned Face

by Stephen Crane

'What will we do now?' said the adjutant,[1] troubled and excited.

'Bury him,' said Timothy Lean.

The two officers looked down close to their toes where lay the body of their comrade. The face was chalk-blue; gleaming eyes stared at the sky. Over the two upright figures was a windy sound of bullets, and on the top of the hill Lean's prostrate company of Spitzbergen infantry[2] was firing measured volleys.

'Don't you think it would be better—' began the adjutant. 'We might leave him until tomorrow.'

'No,' said Lean. 'I can't hold that post an hour longer. I've got to fall back, and we've got to bury old Bill.'

'Of course,' said the adjutant, at once. 'Your men got entrenching tools?'

Lean shouted back to his little line, and two men came slowly, one with a pick, one with a shovel. They started in the direction of the Rostina sharpshooters. Bullets cracked near their ears. 'Dig here,' said Lean gruffly. The men, thus caused to lower their glances to the turf, became hurried and frightened, merely because they could not look to see whence the bullets came. The dull beat of the pick striking the earth

[1] army officer in charge of routine administration.

[2] this does not refer to a specific place; the story is set in an imaginary country in Europe

sounded amid the swift snap of close bullets. Presently the other private began to shovel.

'I suppose,' said the adjutant, slowly, 'we'd better search his clothes for – things.'

Lean nodded. Together in curious abstraction they looked at the body. Then Lean stirred his shoulders suddenly, arousing himself.

'Yes,' he said, 'we'd better see what he's got.' He dropped to his knees, and his hands approached the body of the dead officer. But his hands wavered over the buttons of the tunic. The first button was brick-red with drying blood, and he did not seem to dare touch it.

'Go on,' said the adjutant, hoarsely.

Lean stretched his wooden hand, and his fingers fumbled the bloodstained buttons. At last he rose with ghastly face. He had gathered a watch, a whistle, a pipe, a tobacco-pouch, a handkerchief, a little case of cards and papers. He looked at the adjutant. There was a silence. The adjutant was feeling that he had been a coward to make Lean do all the grisly business.

'Well,' said Lean, 'that's all, I think. You have his sword and revolver?'

'Yes,' said the adjutant, his face working, and then he burst out in a sudden strange fury at the two privates. 'Why don't you hurry up with that grave? What are you doing, anyhow? Hurry, do you hear? I never saw such stupid—'

Even as he cried out in his passion the two men were labouring for their lives. Ever overhead the bullets were spitting.

The grave was finished. It was not a masterpiece – a poor little shallow thing. Lean and the adjutant again looked at each other in a curious silent communication.

Suddenly the adjutant croaked out a weird laugh. It was a terrible laugh, which had its origin in that part of the mind which is first moved by the singing of the nerves, 'Well,' he said humorously to Lean, 'I suppose we had best tumble him in.'

'Yes,' said Lean. The two privates stood waiting, bent over their implements. 'I suppose,' said Lean, 'it would be better if we laid him in ourselves.'

'Yes,' said the adjutant. Then, apparently remembering that he had made Lean search the body, he stooped with great fortitude and took hold of the dead officer's clothing. Lean joined him. Both were particular that their fingers should not feel the corpse. They tugged away; the corpse lifted, heaved, toppled, flopped into the grave, and the two officers, straightening, looked again at each other – they were always looking at each other. They sighed with relief.

The adjutant said, 'I suppose we should – we should say something. Do you know the service, Tim?'

'They don't read the service until the grave is filled in,' said Lean, pressing his lips to an academic expression.

'Don't they?' said the adjutant, shocked that he had made the mistake. 'Oh, well,' he cried, suddenly, 'let us – let us say something – while he can hear us.'

'All right,' said Lean, 'Do you know the service?'

'I can't remember a line of it,' said the adjutant.

Lean was extremely dubious, 'I can repeat two lines, but—'

'Well, do it,' said the adjutant. 'Go as far as you can. That's better than nothing. And the beasts have got our range exactly.'

Lean looked at his two men. 'Attention,' he barked. The privates came to attention with a click, looking much aggrieved. The adjutant lowered his helmet to his knee. Lean, bareheaded, stood over the grave. The Rostina sharpshooters fired briskly.

'O Father, our friend has sunk in the deep waters of death, but his spirit has leaped toward Thee as the bubble arises from the lips of the drowning. Perceive, we beseech, O Father, the little flying bubble, and—'

Lean, although husky and ashamed, had suffered no hesitation up to this point, but he stopped with a hopeless feeling and looked at the corpse.

The adjutant moved uneasily. 'And from Thy superb heights—' he began, and then he too came to an end.

'And from Thy superb heights,' said Lean.

The adjutant suddenly remembered a phrase in the back of the Spitzbergen burial service, and he exploited it with the triumphant manner of a man who has recalled everything, and can go on.

'O God, have mercy—'

'O God, have mercy—' said Lean.

'Mercy,' repeated the adjutant, in quick failure.

'Mercy,' said Lean. And then he was moved by some violence of feeling, for he turned upon his two men and tigerishly said, 'Throw the dirt in.'

The fire of the Rostina sharpshooters was accurate and continuous.

One of the aggrieved privates came forward with his shovel. He lifted his first shovel-load of earth, and for a moment of inexplicable hesitation it was held poised above this corpse, which from its chalk-blue face looked keenly out from the grave. Then the soldier emptied his shovel on – on the feet.

Timothy Lean felt as if tons had been swiftly lifted from off his forehead. He had felt that perhaps the private might empty the shovel on – on the face. It had been emptied on the feet. There was a great point gained there – ha, ha! – the first shovelful had been emptied on the feet. How satisfactory!

The adjutant began to babble. 'Well, of course – a man we've messed with all these years – impossible – you can't, you know, leave your intimate friends rotting on the field. Go on, for God's sake, and shovel, you.'

The man with the shovel suddenly ducked, grabbed his left arm with his right hand, and looked at his officer for orders. Lean picked the shovel from the ground. 'Go to the rear,' he said to the wounded man. He also addressed the other private. 'You get under cover, too; I'll finish this business.'

The wounded man scrambled hard still for the top of the ridge without devoting any glances to the direction from whence the bullets came, and the other man followed at an equal pace; but he was different, in that he looked back anxiously three times.

This is merely the way – often – of the hit and unhit.

Timothy Lean filled the shovel, hesitated, and then, in a movement which was like a gesture of abhorrence, he flung the dirt into the grave, and as it landed it made a sound – plop. Lean suddenly stopped and mopped his brow – a tired labourer.

'Perhaps we have been wrong,' said the adjutant. His glance wavered stupidly. 'It might have been better if we hadn't buried him just at this time. Of course, if we advance tomorrow the body would have been—'

'Damn you,' said Lean, 'shut your mouth.' He was not the senior officer.

He again filled the shovel and flung the earth. Always the earth made that sound – plop. For a space Lean worked frantically, like a man digging himself out of danger.

Soon there was nothing to be seen but the chalk-blue face. Lean filled the shovel. 'Good God,' he cried to the adjutant. 'Why didn't you turn him somehow when you put him in? This—' Then Lean began to stutter.

The adjutant understood. He was pale to the lips. 'Go on, man,' he cried, beseechingly, almost in a shout.

Lean swung back the shovel. It went forward in a pendulum curve. When the earth landed it made a sound – plop.

Summer Flower

by Tamiki Hara
translated by George Saito

On 6 August 1945, at the end of the Second World War, the Americans used a new weapon, the atomic bomb, against Japan. It devastated Hiroshima. The mushroom cloud rose to over 18,000 metres in the sky. Once the cloud cleared, little was left intact. Most of the city was destroyed and more than 70,000 people were killed immediately. Almost the same number again were to succumb to radiation sickness, a new man-made illness. As a result of this, the Japanese surrendered.

I went downtown and bought some flowers, thinking I would visit the grave of my wife. In my pocket I had a bundle of incense sticks that I had taken from the Buddhist[1] altar in my home. August 15 would be the first anniversary for the soul of my wife, but it was doubtful whether my native town would survive until then. Although most factories were closed that day due to electric power rationing, there was no one to be seen except myself – walking along the street with flowers, in the early morning. I did not know the name of the flowers, but they looked like a summer variety with the rustic[2] beauty of their tiny yellow petals.

As I sprayed water over the gravestone exposed to the scorching heat of the sun, divided the flowers into two bunches and put them in the vases on either side, the

[1] a member of the eastern religion founded by the Buddha
[2] simple and unsophisticated, typical of the countryside

grave appeared rather refreshing, and I gazed at the flowers and the stone for a while. Underneath the grave were buried not only the ashes of my wife but also those of my parents. After burning the incense sticks that I had brought and making a bow, I drank out of the well beside the grave. Then I went home by way of Nigitsu Park. The scent of the incense remained in my pocket throughout that day and the next. It was on the third day after my visit to the grave that the bomb was dropped.

My life was saved because I was in the bathroom. On the morning of August 6, I had gotten up around eight o'clock. The air-raid alarm had sounded twice the night before and nothing had happened, so that before dawn I had taken off my clothes and slept in my night robe, which I had not put on for a long time. Such being the case, I had on only my shorts when I got up. My younger sister, when she saw me, complained of my rising late, but I went into the bathroom without replying.

I do not remember how many seconds passed after that. All of a sudden, a powerful blow struck me and darkness fell before my eyes. Involuntarily I shouted and held my hands over my head. Aside from the sound of something like the crashing of a storm, I could not tell what it was in the complete darkness. I groped for the door, opened it, and found the veranda. Until then, I had been hearing my own voice exclaiming. 'Wah!' amid the rushing sounds, agonised at not being able to see. But after I came out to the veranda, the scene of destruction gradually loomed in the dusk before my eyes and I became clearly conscious.

It looked like an episode from a loathsome dream. At first, when the blow struck my head, and I lost my sight, I knew that I had not been killed. Then I became angry, thinking that things had become very troublesome. And my own shouts sounded almost like the voice of somebody else. But when I could see, vaguely as it was, the things around me, I felt as if I were standing stage centre in a tragic play. Certainly I had beheld such a scene in a movie. Beyond the clouds of dust, patches of blue sky began to come into view. Light came in through holes in the walls and from other unexpected directions. As I walked gingerly on the boards where the tatami flooring had been blown off, my sister came rushing toward me. 'You weren't hurt? You weren't hurt? Are you all right? Your eyes are bleeding. Go wash right away.' She told me that there was still water running in the kitchen scullery.

Finding myself completely naked, I turned to my sister and asked her. 'Can you at least get me something to put on?' She was able to pull out a pair of shorts from the closet that had been saved from destruction. Someone rushed in with a bewildered gesture. His face was smeared in blood. He wore only a shirt. This man was an employee of a nearby factory. Seeing me, he said, 'It's lucky you were saved.' Then he bustled away, muttering, 'Telephone ... I have to make a telephone call.'

There were crevices[3] everywhere, and the doors, screens, and tatami mats were scattered about. The pillars and doorsills were clearly exposed, and the whole building was filled with a strange silence. Later I was told that most houses were completely destroyed in that area, but my second floor did not give way; even the floor boards remained firm. My father, a painstaking builder, had built our house about forty years before, and it had been solidly constructed.

Tramping about over the littered mats and screens, I

[3] narrow cracks

looked among scattered articles for something to wear. The book which I had left half read the night before was there on the floor with its pages turned up. The picture frame which had fallen from the beam overhead stood tinged with death in front of the *tokonoma*.[4] I found my canteen quite unexpectedly, and then my hat. Still unable to find my pants, I started looking for something else to cover myself.

K of the factory office appeared on the veranda of the drawing room. Seeing me, he cried in a sad voice, 'I'm hurt! Help me!' and dropped down in a heap where he stood. Blood was oozing from his forehead, and his eyes were glistening with tears.

'Where is it?' I asked, and he distorted his pale wrinkled face, saying, 'My knees,' as he held them with his hand. I gave him a strip of cloth, and I drew over my own legs two pairs of socks, one over the other.

'It's started to smoke. Let's get out of here. Help me get away.' K, who was considerably older than I but usually much more vigorous, seemed to be highly disturbed.

Looking out from the veranda, I could see nothing recognisable except the clusters of flattened houses and a ferroconcrete[5] building a little farther away. Beside the toppled-over mud wall there was a tall maple tree whose trunk was torn off halfway up; the twigs had been thrown into the wash basin. Suddenly K stopped by the air-raid shelter, and said, 'Why don't we stay here? There's a water tank, besides ...' When I said, 'No, let's go to the river,' he asked me wonderingly, 'The river? Which direction is the river?'

[4] also tokonama – an alcove in Japanese houses for scroll painting, flower arrangement and art objects; the most honoured place for a guest to sit is next to the tokonama

[5] strengthened concrete

I took a night robe out of the closet, handed it to him, and tore the shelter curtain. I picked up a cushion, too. When I turned the mat on the veranda, I found my emergency bag. I felt relieved and put the bag on my shoulder. Small red flames rose from the warehouse of the chemical factory next door. We went out over the completely twisted maple.

That tall tree had stood in the corner of the garden for a long time, and had been an object of dreamy imagination in my childhood. Recently I had come back and started living at my own home after a long time, and now I thought it odd that even this tree did not evoke the same old sweet memory. What was strange was that my home town itself had lost its soft natural atmosphere, and I felt it to be something like a composition of cruel, inorganic matter. Every time I went into the drawing room facing the garden, the title, *The Fall of the House of Usher*,[6] spontaneously sprang to my mind.

K and I climbed over the crumbling house, clearing obstacles from our path, and walked slowly at first. We came to level ground, and knew that we were on the road, where we walked faster down the middle. Suddenly there called a voice from behind a crushed building, crying, 'Please!' Turning back, I found that the voice belonged to a woman with a blood-stained face walking toward us. 'Help me!' she cried, following us desperately. We had walked on for some time when we passed an old woman who stood in the middle of the path with her legs wide apart. She was crying like a child, 'The house is catching fire! The house is catching

[6] written by Edgar Allan Poe (1809–49). The narrator visits the crumbling house of his childhood companion, Roderick Usher, to find that both Usher and his twin sister are in the final stages of physical and mental illness.

fire!' Smoke rose here and there from the crumbling houses, and suddenly we came upon a spot where breaths of flame belched furiously.

We passed it running. The road became level again, and we found ourselves at the foot of Sakae Bridge. Here the refugees gathered one after another. Someone who had stationed himself on the bridge cried out: 'Those who are strong enough, put out the fire!' I walked toward the grove of Asano Park, and there became separated from K.

The bamboo grove had been mowed down, and a path made through the grove under the tramping feet of refugees. Most of the trees overhead had been torn apart in mid-air, and this famous old garden on the river was now disfigured with pockmarks[7] and gashes. Beside a hedge was a middle-aged woman, her ample body slumped over limply. Even as I looked, something infectious seemed to emanate from her lifeless face. It was the first such face I had seen. But I was to see many, many more that were more grotesque.

In the grove facing the riverbank I came across a group of students. These girls had escaped from a factory, and all had been injured slightly, but now, trembling from the freshness of the thing that had happened before their very eyes, they chattered excitedly. At that moment my eldest brother appeared. He wore only a shirt, but looked unhurt. He had a beer bottle in one hand. The houses on the other bank of the river had collapsed and were on fire, but the electric poles still stood. Sitting on the narrow road by the riverbank, I felt I was all right now. What had been threatening me, what had been destined to happen, had taken place at last. I could consider myself as one

[7] marked with hollow scars where diseased spots had been

who survived. I have to keep a record of this, I said to myself. But I scarcely knew the truth about the air raid then.

The fire on the opposite bank of the river raged more furiously. The scorching heat reached this side of the river, so that we had to dip the cushion in the rising water and put it over our heads. Then someone shouted, 'Air raid! People with white clothing should hide under the trees!' All the people crowded into the heart of the grove.

The sun sent forth its bright rays, and the other side of the grove seemed to be on fire. A hot wind blew overhead, and black smoke was fanned up toward the middle of the river. Then the sky suddenly grew dark, and large drops came down in torrents. The rain reduced the heat momentarily, but soon the sky cleared up again. The fire on the other bank was still burning. Over on this side, my eldest brother, my younger sister, and a couple of people from our neighbourhood whose faces I recognised had appeared. We got together and talked about what had happened that morning.

My brother had been seated at a table in his office when a flash of light raced through the garden. The next instant, he was blown some distance from his seat and for a while found himself squirming around under the wreckage of the house. At last he discovered an opening and succeeded in crawling out. From the direction of the factory he could hear the student workers screaming for help, and he went off to do what he could to rescue them.

My sister had seen the flash of light from the entrance hall and had rushed as fast as she could to hide under the stairs. As a result, she had suffered little injury.

Everyone had at first thought that just his own house

had been hit by a bomb. But then when they went outside and saw that it was the same everywhere, they were dumbfounded. They were also greatly puzzled by the fact that, although the houses and other buildings had all been damaged or destroyed, there didn't seem to be any holes where the bombs had fallen. The air-raid warning had been lifted, and shortly after that there had been a big flash of light and a soft hissing sound like magnesium burning. The next they knew everything was turned upside down. It was all like some kind of magical trick, my sister said, trembling with terror.

The fire on the opposite bank had no sooner begun to die down when someone said that the trees in the garden on this side of the river had caught fire. We could see wisps of smoke rising in the sky behind the grove. The water in the river remained at high tide and did not recede.

I walked along a stone embankment down to the water's edge and discovered a large wooden box floating along at my feet, and around it bobbed onions that had spilled out. Pulling the box to me, I took out the onions and handed them to people on the bank. The box had been thrown out of a freight train which had been overturned on the bridge upstream. While I was picking up the onions, there came a voice crying, 'Help!' Clinging to a scrap of wood, a young girl drifted in the middle of the river, floating at one moment and sinking at another. I took a large piece of timber and swam toward her pushing it. Although I had not swum for a long time, I managed to help her more easily than I had expected.

The fire on the opposite bank, which had slackened for a while, had started raging again. This time, murky smoke mingled with the red flames, and as the roiling mass expanded, the heat of the flames seemed to grow more intense with each second. When the fire finally burned itself out, there remained only an empty carcass. It was then that I sensed a wall of air undulating toward us over the water. Tornado! Even as the thought struck me, a blast of wind passed over our heads. The grass and trees around me trembled, and whole trees were plucked out and snatched high into the air. I don't remember exactly what colour the air around us was at that time. I think it must have been wrapped in a kind of weird greenish glow, the kind you see in pictures of Hell.

When the tornado had passed, the sky showed that evening was near. My second elder brother appeared quite unexpectedly. His shirt was torn in back, and there was a brushing trace the colour of thin India ink on his face which later became a suppurating[8] burn. Coming home on business, he had sighted a small aeroplane in the sky and then three strange flashes. After being thrown on the ground, he had run to rescue his wife and the maid-servant, who were struggling under the collapsed house. He entrusted his two children to the maid and let them escape before him, and then spent much time in saving the old man who lived next door.

His wife had been worrying about the children who had gone off with the maid when she heard the maid shouting to her from the opposite bank. The maid said her arms hurt so much she couldn't carry the children any longer and she wanted someone to come and help her right away.

The grove of Asano Park was little by little catching fire. If night came on and the fire reached the part of

[8] producing pus (from a wound)

the grove where we were, we would be in trouble, so we thought we had better cross over to the other bank while it was still light. But where we were there was no boat to ferry us across. My eldest brother and his group decided to go around by way of the bridge, but my second elder brother and I walked upstream, still hoping to find a ferryboat. The sinking sun made everything around us look pale, and both on and beneath the bank there were pale people who cast their sinister shadows on the water. Their faces were so puffy and swollen you could hardly tell whether they were men or women, with eyes that were mere slits and horribly blistered lips. They lay on their sides, their painful limbs exposed, barely breathing. When we passed before them, these strange people spoke to us in faint, gentle voices, 'Give us some water.'

Someone called me in a sharp, pitiful voice. Below I saw a naked young boy whose lifeless body was completely sunk in the water, and two women squatting on the stone steps less than four feet from the corpse. Their faces were swollen twice their natural size, distorted in an ugly way, and only their scorched rumpled hair showed that they were women. Looking at them, I shuddered rather than felt pity. But the women had noticed me. 'That mattress over by those trees is ours. Would you be good enough to bring it over here?' they pleaded.

Looking over at the trees, I saw that there was in fact a mattress there. But a man who looked like he was mortally wounded was lying on it, so there was nothing I could do.

My brother and I found a little raft, untied the rope, and rowed toward the opposite bank of the river. Daylight had already turned dusky when the raft reached the sand beach on the other side, and the area was scattered with wounded townsmen. A soldier who was squatting by the river said to me, 'Let me drink some hot water.' I had him lean against my shoulder and we walked together. As he staggered on the sand, the soldier muttered, 'It's much better to be killed.' I made him wait beside the path.

Nearing a water supply station I beheld the large burned head of a human being slowly drinking hot water out of a cup; the enormous face seemed to be made up of black soybeans; and the hair above the ears was burned off in a straight line where the man's cap had not protected it. I filled a cup and took it to the soldier. As I did so, I saw another soldier, badly wounded, down on his knees in the river, bending over and intently lapping up the river water.

People were starting to cook their supper, burning pieces of wood on the sandy beach. For some time now, I had been aware of a girl with a terribly swollen face lying close by my side and begging for water. After a while, it dawned on me that it was the maid from my second elder brother's house, the one who had gone off with the children and had earlier been calling for help. She had just been going out the kitchen door with the baby strapped on her back when the blinding flash had come and her face and hands and breast had been burned. My brother had sent her off ahead of him with the baby and the older girl, but when she got to the bridge, she somehow lost the older girl. Still carrying the baby, she had made her way down here to the riverbed. When the flash came, she had held up her hand to shield her face, and now the hand hurt her so much she felt like tearing it off, she said.

As the tide began to rise, we all moved up the bank. Night had fallen, and a breeze sprang up. It was too cool for us to sleep, and we kept hearing voices here and there crying desperately for water. Nigitsu Park was nearby but it was now wrapped in darkness, and we could see only faintly the broken trees. My brothers lay in a hollow in the ground and I placed myself in another shallow place. Close to me lay three or four wounded schoolgirls. 'The grove over there has started burning,' someone said. 'Don't you think we'd better move away from here?' Getting out of the hollow, I saw flames glaring over the top of the trees ahead of us, but there was no sign of the fire spreading up to our spot.

'Does it look as though the fire is going to come over this way?' a wounded girl asked in a frightened voice. When I assured her it was all right, she said, 'I wonder what time it is now. Do you think it's twelve o'clock yet?'

There must still have been an undamaged siren somewhere, for we heard its warning faint in the distance.

'I wish morning would come!' one of the schoolgirls complained.

A chorus of soft voices could be heard calling, 'Mother! Father!' 'Does it look as though the fire is coming over this way?' the wounded girl asked again.

From the direction of the riverbed came death cries, in a young voice still strong. 'Water! Water! Please . . .! Mother . . . Sister . . . Mitchan . . .!' The agonised words, interspersed with moans and weak gasps of pain, seemed to wrench his whole body. One time when I was little I walked along the embankment here and came to the riverbed to catch fish. The memory of that hot summer day remains strangely vivid in my mind. There was a big billboard stuck up in the sand advertising Lion toothpaste, and every now and then from the direction of the railway bridge came the rumble of a passing train. It was a peaceful scene that now seemed like a dream.

By the time morning came, the voices from the night before had ceased, though the piercing death cries that had wrung my heart still rang in my ears. As the scene gradually brightened, a morning breeze began to blow. My eldest brother and my sister went off in the direction where our house had stood, saying they would make their way from there to the East Parade Ground, having heard that a dispensary[9] had been set up there. My second elder brother and his family started off for the East Parade Ground too. I was about to set out for the parade ground myself, when a soldier nearby asked if I would take him with me. He was a big man, and he must have been badly wounded, because he hung on my shoulder and dragged his feet gingerly along the ground as though they were broken things. We had to pick our way among formidable obstacles, shattered glass here, corpses there, objects that were still hot and smouldering. By the time we got to Tokiwa Bridge, the soldier said he was too exhausted to go another step and asked me to leave him there. I did as he told me and went off alone in the direction of Nigitsu Park.

Here and there were houses that had collapsed but had escaped the fire, and everywhere were the scars of that flash of light that had raked over the scene. In an empty lot a crowd of people had gathered. A trickle of water was leaking from the water main. It was there that I chanced to learn that my niece – my second elder brother's child who had gotten separated from the maid yesterday – was safe at the refugee area in the Tōshōgū Shrine.

I hurried off to the garden of the shrine, and came on my little niece just as she and her mother had found each other. The day before, after becoming separated

[9] place where medicine is given out

from the maid at the bridge, she had gone off with some other people and made her way here. Now, when she caught sight of her mother, the strain was suddenly too much for her and she burst out wailing. Her head was black and painful-looking from burns.

A dispensary had been established near the entrance to the Tōshōgū Shrine. With each case a policeman formally asked the patient his permanent address and age; and the patient, even after receiving a slip of paper identifying him, still had to wait about an hour in a long row, under the scorching sun. Patients who were able to join that row were more fortunate than the rest. Now someone cried furiously, 'Soldier! Soldier! Help me! Soldier!' A horribly burned young girl rolled in anguish on the roadside. And near her was a man in the uniform of an air defence guard, who complained in feeble voice, 'Please help me, ah, Nurse, Doctor!' as he laid his head, swollen and bloated with burns, on a stone, and opened his blackened mouth. No one gave heed to him. Policemen, doctors, and nurses came from other towns to help, but they were rather few in number.

The maid from my elder brother's family had come to the dispensary with my brother and I helped her to join the row of persons awaiting treatment. Her face and hands were getting more and more swollen and she seemed to want to squat on the ground. When her turn finally came and she had finished being treated, we had to look around for some place to rest. Everywhere we looked in the grounds of the shrine there were wounded people, but there was nothing like a tent or a thicket of trees where we could take shelter. Finally we propped some thin pieces of lumber up against the stone fence surrounding the shrine to make a kind of roof and crawled in under them. For the next twenty-four hours, this cramped space was home for the six of us, my second elder brother and his wife, their two girls, the maid and myself.

Right next to us someone had set up a similar kind of shelter where a man moved around briskly on a piece of matting. Presently he struck up a conversation with us. He had no shirt or undershirt, and all that was left of his trousers was a piece around his waist and part of one leg. His arms, his legs and his face were burned. He said he had been on the seventh floor of the Chūgoku Building when the explosion came, and we could see he had been injured in the blast. He must have had great presence of mind, however, as he had asked people to help him and had somehow managed to flee all the way here.

About that time, a young man with a military cadet's[10] belt, his body smeared all over with blood, pushed his way into the man's shelter. The man was incensed. 'Here, here! Get out of here! As sore as I am, I'm not going to have you bumping into me! There're any number of other places you can go – why do you want to squeeze in here! Come on now, get out!' he spluttered in a voice like a bark. The blood-smeared youth got to his feet with a dazed look.

A few yards away from us, two schoolgirls lay groaning for water under a cherry tree, faces burned black, their thin shoulders exposed to the scorching sun. They were students of the girls' commercial school who had met the disaster while potato digging in the vicinity. A woman in work trousers with a smoke-shrivelled face joined them. Placing her handbag on the ground, she stretched out her legs listlessly, oblivious to the dying girls. The day was drawing to a close. When I

[10] young person training for the armed forces or police

thought of spending another night in a place like this, I became strangely uneasy.

The second night dragged by. Before dawn some unknown voice took up a Buddhist invocation,[11] a sound suggesting that people were dying all the time. The two commercial students died when the morning sun was high. A policeman, when he had finished examining the girls' bodies lying face down in the ditch, approached the dead woman in work trousers nearby. He opened her handbag and found a savings passbook and public loan bonds in it. She still wore the travelling suit in which she had been struck.

About noon, the air-raid warning sounded again and the roar of planes was heard. Although I had become used to the ugliness and misery around me, my fatigue and hunger became more and more intense. My second elder brother's two sons were off at school in the city when the disaster occurred and we still did not know what had happened to them. People died one after another, and their bodies were left as they were. Men walked restlessly, without hope of assistance.

The desperate clarion call[12] of the bugle came from the parade ground. Meanwhile, my brother's little girls sobbed miserably from their burns and the maid kept constantly begging for water. And then, just as I thought we were coming to the end of our endurance, my eldest brother appeared. He had stopped the previous day at Hatsukaichi, to which his sister-in-law had evacuated, and had hired a wagon. He was here with the wagon now, ready to take us away.

My second elder brother, his family, my sister, who had meanwhile joined us, and I all got in the wagon

[11] prayer
[12] high-pitched trumpet sound

and we left the Tōshōgū Shrine and went toward Nigitsu. As we were going from Shirashima past the entrance of Asano Garden, my second elder brother caught sight of a body in the vacant lot toward the West Parade Ground. It was clothed in yellow pants that were familiar to him. It was Fumihiko, his son. Fluid flowed from a swelling on the boy's breast the size of a fist. His white teeth were dimly visible in his blackened face, and the fingers of both hands were bent inward with the nails boring into the skin. Beside him sprawled the body of a schoolboy and that of a young woman. They lay slightly apart. Both had become rigid in their last positions. My second elder brother stripped off Fumihiko's nails and his belt for a keepsake. Placing a name card on him, we left the spot. It was an encounter too sad for tears.

The wagon then passed Kokutaiji Temple and Sumiyoshi Bridge, and came to Koi, giving me an almost full view of the burned sites of the busiest quarters. Amid the vast, silvery expanse of nothingness that lay under the glaring sun, there were the roads, the river, the bridges, and the stark-naked, swollen bodies. The limbs of these corpses, which seemed to have become rigid after struggling in their last agony, had a kind of haunting rhythm. In the scattered electric wires and countless wrecks there was embodied a spasmodic design in nothingness. The burnt and toppled streetcar and the horse with its huge belly on the ground gave me the impression of a world described by a Dali surrealist painting.[13] The tall camphor tree in the precincts of Kokutaiji Temple had been felled completely, and the gravestones too were scattered. The Asano Library,

[13] Salvador Dali (1904–89) was a Spanish artist who painted nightmare worlds in realistic detail

with only its outer block left, had been turned into a morgue. The roads were still smoky here and there and were permeated with a cadaverous[14] smell. Somehow it seems that impressions of the scene are more aptly put in *katakana*:[15]

> The strange rhythm of the human bodies,
>   inflamed and red,
> That mingle with the glaring wrecks
>   and the cinders of greyish white
> In the vast panorama –
> Is this all that has happened, or is it
>   what could have happened?
> Oh, the world stripped of all in an
>   instant.
> How the swollen belly of the horse
>   glares beside the toppled streetcar.
> And the stench of the smouldering wires!

The wagon proceeded along the endless road through the debris. Even on the outskirts of the city, the houses all had collapsed, and it was only after we had passed Kusatsu that we were at last liberated from the shadow of disaster and were greeted by the sight of living green. The appearance of the dragonflies that flitted so swiftly above the emerald rice paddies was touchingly refreshing to my eyes. From here stretched a long, monotonous road to Yawata Village. Night had fallen by the time we reached there and all was dismally quiet.

The next day, our miserable life – of the aftermath – truly began. The wounded did not recover satisfactorily,

[14] a cadaver is a corpse; cadaverous means deathly pale, or can refer to the smell of death

[15] katakana characters are much simpler and sharper in appearance than other figures in Japanese writing

and even those who at first had been strong gradually grew weak from lack of food. Our maid's arm suppurated badly, and flies gathered around the burned part, which finally became infested with maggots. No matter how often we sterilised the area, the maggots never ceased to infest the wound. She died a little more than a month later.

Four or five days after we had moved to the village, my nephew, who had been last seen on his way to school, suddenly reappeared. On the morning that he had gone to his school – his building later was to be evacuated – he had seen the flash from inside his classroom. In an instant he hid himself under the desk, and was buried under the falling ceiling, but crawled out through a crevice. There were only four or five boys who had escaped – the rest were killed by the first blow. The survivors ran toward Hiji Hill, and he vomited white fluid on the way. Then he went to the home of one of his friends with whom he had escaped, and there he was sheltered. About a week after his return, my nephew's hair began to fall out, and his nose bled. His doctor declared that his condition was already critical, but my nephew gradually regained his strength.

My friend N suffered a different experience. He was on his way to visit an evacuated factory, and his train had just entered a tunnel. As the train came out, he saw three parachutes floating down through the air over Hiroshima several miles behind. Arriving at the next station, he was surprised to find that the window panes were broken. By the time he reached his destination, detailed information already had been circulated. He took the first train back to Hiroshima. Every train that passed was filled with people grotesquely wounded. When he arrived at the city, he could not wait until the fire was out, and so he proceeded along the still hot asphalt road.

He went first to the girls' high school where his wife taught. On the site of the classrooms lay the bones of the pupils, and on the site of the principal's office lay bones that seemed to have belonged to the principal. Nothing could he identify as the remains of his wife. He hurried back to his own home. Being near Ujina, the house had crumbled without burning. Yet he could not find his wife there either. Then he examined all the bodies lying on the road that led from his home to the girls' school. Most of the bodies were lying on their faces, so that he had to turn them over with his hands in order to examine them. Every woman had been changed miserably, but his wife's body was not there. Finally he wandered around without direction. He saw some ten bodies heaped in a pile in a cistern.

Then there were three bodies that had become rigid as they held a ladder set against the riverbank, and others stood waiting in a line for the bus, the nails of each fastened on the shoulders of the one ahead. The terrible scene of the West Parade Ground was beyond description. There were piles of soldier corpses all around – but the body of his wife was not to be found anywhere.

My friend N visited all the barracks, and looked into the faces of the severely wounded people. Every face was miserable beyond words, but none of the faces was his wife's. After looking for three days and nights at so many charred bodies, dead and living, N at last went back to the burned site of his wife's school.

The Alien Skull

by Liam O'Flaherty

When he was within ten yards of the enemy outpost, Private Mulhall lay flat, with his right ear close to the ground. He listened without drawing breath. He strained his ear to catch a word, a cough, or the grating sound of a boot touching the frost-bound earth. There was no sound.

Had they gone?

It was eleven o'clock at night. There was perfect silence along that section of the battle-front. In the distance there was the monotonous and melancholy murmur of heavy guns in action. Here everything was still, as in a tomb. The moon had not risen. But the sky was not dark. It was an angry blue colour. There were stars. It was possible to see the ground for a long distance. It was freezing heavily. Bayonets, lying beside dead men, gleamed. All the huddled figures scattered about between the two lines of trenches were dead men. There had been a battle that day.

They had sent out Mulhall to discover whether the enemy had retired from his front line. If so, an advance was to be made at midnight into the trenches evacuated by him. If possible, Mulhall was to bring back a live prisoner. A man had been seen a little earlier peering over the top of the advanced post, before which Mulhall was now lying.

Irritated by the silence, Mulhall began to curse under his breath. He had ceased to listen and looked back towards his own line. He had come up a slope. He saw the dim shapes of the newly made scattered posts, the rambling wire fences and the heaps of rooted earth. He cursed and felt a savage hatred against his officers. He had now been three years at the front without leave. He was always doing punishment behind the line for insolence and insubordination. In the line he was chosen for every dangerous duty, because of his ferocious courage. But as soon as he came out he was up again before the adjutant, taken dirty on parade, absent, drunk, or for striking a corporal.

Lying flat on the ground, Mulhall thought savagely of the injustice done to him. He thought with cunning pleasure of crawling back towards his own line and shooting one of the officers or sergeants against whom he had a grudge. With pleasure, he rehearsed, in his mind, this act, until he saw the stricken victim fall, writhe, and lie still. Then terrible disciplinary[1] cries rose up before his mind, his own name shouted by the sergeant, and then the giant figure of the sergeant-major, with his pace stick under his arm, heels together, erect, reading out the documentary evidence. A whole lot of shouting and stamping and awe-inspiring words. An enormous, invisible, inhuman machine, made of terrible words, constituted in his mind the terror that gave power to his superiors over him.

Compared to that it was pleasant out here.

He turned his head and looked towards the enemy outpost again. His hatred was now directed against the enemy. Their words were meaningless. Whenever he heard their words, they sounded like the barking of a dog. He was not afraid of them, and his punishment was remitted[2] when he killed one or two of them.

[1] punishment as a result of bad behaviour
[2] cancelled

Now he ceased to think and he thrust upwards his lower lip. His body became rigid. He fondled the breech of his rifle. With his rifle folded in his arms, ready for use, he slowly pushed his body forward, moving on his left side. He propelled himself with his left foot. He was listening intently. He moved like a snail, a few inches at a time. He made no sound. Then he stopped suddenly when he had gone half the distance. He had heard a sound. It was the sound of teeth gnawing a crust of hard bread, an army biscuit or a stale piece of bread, hardened by the frost. An enemy! There was an enemy there in front, five yards away.

He turned over gently on his stomach and brought his rifle to the front. Then he slowly touched various parts of his equipment and of his weapon to see that everything was in order. He settled his steel hat a little farther forward on his head, so that its rim shielded his face. Then he raised his back until he was on his elbows and knees. He then raised his feet and hands. He crawled forward as slowly as before and even more silently, breathing gently through his nose. He reached the post and lay still, behind a little knoll that formed the parapet. The enemy was within a yard of him. The enemy snuffled as he chewed at the crust.

Mulhall slowly raised his right knee. He put his right foot to the ground under him. He balanced his rifle in his right hand. He put his left hand on the ground. Then he jumped. He jumped right on top of the man in the hole beyond. But his foot struck something hard as he fell downwards and he tumbled over the man, losing his rifle. His head struck the side of the hole. He was slightly dazed. Almost immediately, however, he raised himself and held out his hands to grope for the enemy.

The enemy had also been tossed by the impact. Just

then he was pulling himself up against the side of the hole, his hands supporting him, his mouth and eyes wide open with fright and wonder. There was a piece of black bread in his right hand. There were crumbs on his lips. His face was within a few inches of Mulhall's face.

Mulhall's hands, which he had thrust forward instinctively to grapple with the enemy, instinctively dropped. With the amazing courage of stupid men, Mulhall saw at a glance that the enemy was much bigger and stronger than himself and that he was almost standing up. Mulhall, on the other hand, was huddled on the ground. Now the enemy was incapable of movement through the paralysis of sudden fear. But if Mulhall touched him the same terror would make him struggle like a madman. Mulhall knew that and lay still. His face imitated the enemy's face. He opened his mouth and dilated his eyes.

They remained motionless, watching one another, like two strange babies. Their rifles lay side by side at the bottom of the hole. The enemy's rifle had been leaning against the side of the hole, and Mulhall had tripped over it, losing his own rifle. Now they were both unarmed. Their faces were so close together that they could hear one another's breathing.

The enemy was a stripling, but fully grown, and of a great size. His cheeks were red and soft. So were his lips. His whole body was covered with good, soft flesh. Mulhall was a squat fellow, thin and hard. His face was pale and marked with scars. He had eyes like a ferret. A drooping, fair moustache covered his lip and curled into his mouth. He looked brutal, ugly, war-worn and humpy compared to the fine young enemy, whose flesh was still soft and fresh on his big limbs.

Although his mouth lay stupidly open, as if with

terror, Mulhall's mind remained brutal, calm, and determinedly watching for an opportunity to capture the enemy. If he could only reach his gun or disengage his entrenching tool or release his jack-knife. But he must take the fellow alive and drag him back over the frosty ground by the scruff of the neck, prodding him with his bayonet.

Then the enemy did a curious thing that completely puzzled Mulhall. At first his face broke into a smile. Then he laughed outright, showing his teeth that were sound and white, like the teeth of a negro. He made a low, gurgling sound when he laughed. Then, slowly, with a jerky, spasmodic movement, he raised the hand that held the crust until the bread was in front of Mulhall's face. Then his face became serious again and his expression changed.

The look of fear left his eyes. They became soft and friendly. His lips trembled. Then his whole body trembled. Gesticulating with his hands and shoulders, he offered the bread to Mulhall eagerly. He moved his lips and made guttural sounds[3] which Mulhall did not understand. Every other time that Mulhall heard those words he thought they were like the barking of a dog. But now they had a different sound.

Mulhall became confused and ashamed. His forehead wrinkled. At first, he felt angry with the enemy, because he had aroused a long-buried feeling of softness. Then he became suspicious. Was the bread poisoned? No. The enemy had been eating it himself. Then he suddenly wanted to shed tears. He thought, with maudlin self-pity, of the brutal callousness and cruelty of his own comrades and superiors. Everybody despised Mulhall. Nobody would share blankets with

[3] sound produced from the back of the throat, harsh sounding

him in the hut. He always got the dregs of the tea. They moved away from him in the canteen. When he was tied to the wheel of the cook-house cart fellows used to jeer at him and cry out: 'Are they bitin' ye, Mull?' With tears in his eyes, Mulhall wanted to bite the hand that held out the bread. The action brought to a climax the whole ghastly misery of his existence. It robbed him of his only solace, the power to hate somebody whom he could injure with impunity.[4]

He was on the point of striking away the bread when his instinct of cunning warned him. So he took the bread. He fumbled with it uncertainly. Then he stuffed it into the pocket of his tunic. The enemy became delighted and made fresh gestures, gabbling all the while.

Then the enemy stopped gabbling and both became still, watching one another. Their faces became suspicious again. Their eyes wandered over one another's bodies, each strange to the other. Their features became hostile. Their hands jerked uneasily.

Mulhall, slightly unnerved by the enemy's action, began to feel afraid. He became acutely conscious of the enemy's size. So he also began to make guttural sounds imitating the enemy. He touched the enemy's sleeve and said: 'Huh. Yuh. Uh. Uh.' Then he put his finger in his mouth and sucked it. Then he nodded his head eagerly. The enemy looked on in wonder, with suspicion in his eyes.

Mulhall took off his steel hat. There was a crumpled cigarette in the hat. He took out the cigarette and gave it to the enemy.

The enemy's face relaxed again. He was overcome with emotion. He took the cigarette and then kissed

[4] without punishment or unpleasant consequences

Mulhall's hand.

Then Mulhall surrendered completely to this extraordinary new feeling of human love and kindness. Were it not for his native[5] sense of reserve, he would return the enemy's kiss. Instead of that he smiled like a happy child and his head swam. He took the enemy's hand and pressed it three times, mumbling something inaudible. They sat in silence for a whole minute, looking at one another in a state of ecstasy. They loved one another for that minute, as saints love God or as lovers love, in the first discovery of their exalted passion. They were carried up from the silent and frightful corpse-strewn battle-field into some God-filled place, into that dream state where life almost reaches the secret of eternal beauty.

They were startled from their ecstasy by the booming of a single cannon, quite near, to the rear of the enemy lines. They heard the whizzing of the shell over their heads, flying afar.

The enemy soldier started. His face grew stern. He sat up on his heels and took Mulhall's hand. He began to make guttural sounds as he pressed Mulhall's hand fervently.

Mulhall also awoke, but slowly. His soul had sunk deeply into the tender reverie of human love so alien to him. Like a sick man awaking from a heavy sleep, he scanned the enemy's face, seeking the meaning of the change that had been caused by the boom and the whizzing passage of the shell. Slowly he became aware of the boom. Then his cunning awoke in him. Was it a signal?

Without changing his features he became cruel again.

[5] inborn, natural

Still uttering guttural sounds, the enemy crawled out into the bottom of the hole and picked up his rifle. Mulhall struggled between the desire of his cunning to throttle the enemy while his back was turned, and an almost identical desire to throw his arms around the enemy's neck and beg him to remain. The cunning desire lost in the struggle and he felt very lonely and miserable as if he were on the point of losing somebody he had loved all his life. So he remained motionless, watching the enemy with soft eyes. And yet he felt violently angry at not being able to hate the enemy and throttle him.

Having taken up his rifle, the enemy paused and looked at the crumpled cigarette which he still held in his hand. Then he smiled and began to make effusive[6] gestures. He kissed the cigarette. Then he made curious sounds, his face aglow with joy and friendship. Then he put down his rifle, pointed to Mulhall's helmet and then to his own. He laughed. He took off his own helmet, which was shaped differently from Mulhall's helmet.

Immediately, Mulhall started violently. He became rigid. All his savagery and brutality again returned. The enemy's skull was exposed. As soon as he saw it the lust of blood overwhelmed him, as if he were a beast of prey in sight of his quarry. The enemy's bare skull acted on his senses like a maddening drug. Its shape was alien. It was shaped like a bullet. It had whitish hairs on it. It was hostile, foreign, uncouth, the mark of the beast. The sight of it caused his blood to curdle in him. A singing sound started in his head, at the rear of his forehead. His eyes glittered. He wanted to kill. He again felt exalted, gripped by the fury of despair.

[6] openly emotional

The skull disappeared. The enemy put his helmet back on his head and then peered over the top of the hole in both directions. Then he struck his chest a great blow, murmured something, and crawled out back towards his own line.

As quick as a cat Mulhall pounced on his own rifle and arranged the breech.[7] Then he crouched up against the side of the hole, thrust out his rifle and looked. The enemy was already a few yards away, slouching off in a stooping position. Quickly, taking quick aim, Mulhall fired. The enemy grunted, stopped, and expanded his chest. Then he turned his head towards Mulhall as he sank slowly. Baring his teeth, with glittering eye, Mulhall aimed slowly at the wondering, gaping young face of the enemy. He fired. The enemy's face twitched and lowered to the ground. His whole body lowered to the ground, trembled and lay still. The haunches[8] remained high off the ground. The feet were drawn up. One hand was thrown out. The head was twisted around towards Mulhall. The face, now stained with blood, still seemed to look at Mulhall with awe and wonder.

Mulhall suddenly felt an irresistible desire to run away.

He dashed out of the hole in the direction of his own line, careless of taking cover. He had not gone three yards when he threw up his hands and dropped his gun. He got it right between the shoulder blades. Coughing and cursing, he fell backwards on his buttocks. His head was still erect. With maniacal joy he looked up into the cruel blue sky and laughed out fierce blasphemies.[9]

[7] prepared the rifle for firing
[8] part of the body from the waist to the thighs
[9] curses, speaking evil against God

They got him again, three times, around the shoulders and neck. His head fell forward. In that position he lay still, like a grotesque statue, dead.

At dawn, when the sun began to shine, he was still sitting that way, like a Turk at prayer, stiff and covered with frost.

The Making of Me

by Robert Westall

You see the state I'm in now, as I sit here.

Do not blame me. My grandfather made me what I am.

With one blow. In one minute.

I had a happy childhood, except for one thing. I hated being 'left with' people, when my parents went off somewhere. You could never tell what people would *do* with you, once your parents had gone.

Like my holy aunt, for instance. No sooner had my parents waved goodbye than one of her holy friends would turn up, hold my head between her hands, look deep into my eyes and ask if I said my prayers and hoped to go to heaven? I mean, what do you *say*?

Other times my aunt, who was Sally Army,[1] would take me off round the streets, marching with the band. I quite liked the band, though I hated the way people stared at us. Especially when we stopped on some wet and windy corner and the Major began shouting wildly about Jesus Christ and Salvation, to the two men and a dog who'd stopped to listen.

He lisped. He kept asking people if they were 'thaved' or were still wallowing in their 'thins'. Some of my mates from school saw me standing next to him once, and I was regularly asked in the playground if I'd

[1] Salvation Army – a Christian organisation founded by William Booth in 1865. Its members wear uniforms.

been 'thaved' from my 'thins'. For a whole three years, till I went to grammar school.

My unholy aunt wasn't so bad. She might condemn God non-stop, for letting little children die of diphtheria[2] or for sinking ships in storms, but at least she stayed home to do it, with nobody to hear but me. And she kept very good chocolate biscuits.

The person I really dreaded being left with, though, was my grandfather. He was not a *person,* like my mum and dad, or my little round laughing nana. He towered above me, six feet tall. I would sometimes glance up at him, as one might peer up in awe at a mountainous crag. The huge nose, the drooping moustache, the drooping mass of wrinkles. Then his eyes would peer down at me, too small, too close together, pale blue, wild and empty of everything but an everlasting, baffled rage. And my own eyes would scurry for cover, like a scared rabbit. He never spoke to me, and I never spoke to him, and thank God my parents never forced me to, as they would force me sometimes to kiss hairy-chinned old ladies.

There were old tales of his violence. How when his second child was born dead, he ripped the gas-cooker from the wall and threw it downstairs (and gas-cookers were solid cast-iron then, and weighed a ton). How when he came home drunk on a Saturday night, Nana and my eleven-year-old father would hear his step and run to hide in the outside wash-house, till he fell into a drunken sleep before the fire. And then Nana would stealthily rifle his pockets for the remains of his week's wages, and go straight and buy the week's shopping before he woke. And when he woke, he would think he'd lost all his money in his drunken stupor.

[2] a contagious disease that starts in the throat

But the Great War[3] had done for him. Unlike anybody else I knew, he had a Chest, because he'd been gassed in the trenches. His Chest made a fascinating symphony of noises at the best of times. So I would listen to it, rather than the chat round the meal-table. But when he was upstairs in bed, bad with his Chest, the whole house was silent and doom-laden, and my parents tiptoed about and talked in whispers.

He was also shell-shocked. Nana always had to be careful with the big black kettle she kept simmering on the hob to make a cup of tea. If it was allowed to boil, the lid would begin to rattle, making exactly the same noise as a distant machine-gun. And that would be enough to send him off into one of his 'dos', when he would imagine he was back in the hell of the trenches and would shout despairing orders, and I would be sent out for a walk till one of his powders settled him.

They said he had killed an Austrian soldier in a bayonet fight and taken his cap-badge. I was sometimes allowed to handle the strange square badge, to keep me quiet. It had a picture in brass of charging infantrymen,[4] and strange, eastern, Hungarian writing. When Granda was *really* bad, he thought the dead Austrian had come back for his badge.

And, above all, he still drank. Perhaps to drown the memories he never spoke of. Oh, the silent agony of waiting to eat Sunday lunch, because of him, at our house; my mother fretting and the painful smell of good roast beef being singed to a crisp in the oven. Every ear cocked for his wavering footsteps. The strange bits of French songs or German marches that he would hum while he pushed his food unwanted round his plate.

[3] the First World War (1914–18)
[4] foot soldiers

Afterwards he would fall asleep with his mouth open. There was never any blackness for me like the blackness of the inside of his mouth.

But, while my parents were there, and the Nana I loved, he was just a fascinating monster, a fabulous beast. Safe to watch, like a tiger in a cage.

But being left alone with him ...

A dreadful silence always fell. Perhaps he thought he had nothing in his mind fit for a child's ears. And my childish prattle, which so made the other grown-ups laugh, just got on his shell-shocked nerves.

Once, without warning, he clouted me across the ear, I think I wasn't so much hurt as *outraged.* Nobody had ever hit me, except my father twice, and that after plenty of warnings. The unfairness of it made the world reel about me. He told my father, afterwards, that I turned to him with tears in my eyes and said,

'Why did you hit me, grandfather?'

It sounds like something out of a Victorian novelette.[5] But it must have cut him to his shell-shocked heart. When my parents returned they found me barricaded safely inside the outside loo, and him rocking with his head in his hands, full of agonised remorse that he had hit that innocent bairn.[6] And vowing never to do it again till the day he died, or might his hand wither and drop off.

The innocent bairn wasn't slow to make the most of such an opening. Next time I was left with him, I found him still silent, but strangely obedient. I soon grasped he would do anything I wanted, just to keep me happy.

To be honest, I don't think I meant to be cruel: I

[5] short story or novel of moderate length, usually a romance, written during the reign of Queen Victoria (1837–1901)

[6] Scottish for child

wasn't a cruel child. But I had suffered a kind of personal earthquake at his hands, and I was very keen to prove his present mood would last, and the earthquake wouldn't happen again.

And I had a hopeless yearning to imitate my father, who was the engineer at the gasworks, and to me, a great wizard who dwelt among roaring furnaces and stamping carthorses, among great heaps of smoking slag and clouds of green gas, and who could start great steel dinosaurs of engines with one push of his small shoulder to an eight foot flywheel.

I wanted to make a *machine*. A machine of brass and steel that swung rhythmically and jangled loudly, and flashed with steel and brass.

I asked Granda to get Nana's washing-line.

He did.

I asked that he string it round the room from the hook on the kitchen door where her apron hung, to the rail above the kitchen range where she dried her tea-towels; from the handle of the cupboard to the hooks on the Welsh dresser. When it was firmly secured, we proceeded to hang from it every pot, pan, ladle and spoon in her well-stocked kitchen.

I pulled on the line. Everything swung, danced, jangled with the most satisfying cacophony.[7] It was like entering into a new world.

Two hours later they found me still happily pulling and clanging, with my grandfather cowering in the depths of his chair with his hands pressed over his shell-shocked ears.

He had kept his word; he had not laid a hand on the innocent bairn. I don't know why he didn't strangle me; it must have been a close-run thing. Even I was

[7] harsh, unharmonious sound

scared at what I'd done – afterwards. When I saw the look on my father's face.

And then my unholy aunt fell ill, and was rushed to hospital and not expected to live. Suddenly the family were going to see her every night, and my mother thought that hospital was no place to take a child. From now on I was going to be left with my grandfather not once a month, but every night. A terrifying desert of silence and strangeness stretched before me. If I'd had any pity to spare from myself, I might have pitied Granda. But I was just plain terrified. What were we going to *say*? What were we going to *do* in that desert of time? I went, that first evening, thinking the end of the world, so often foretold by my holy aunt, was upon me.

I settled myself in the deepest chair, behind a mass of old comics I'd read ten times already. But the *Wizard* (and the famous Wilson, who had run the three-minute mile at the Berlin Olympics when he was a hundred and twenty years old, because he lived on rare herbs) had no charms that night.

I furtively eyed my strange sighing Beast as his chest made its odd symphony of noises, and the terrifying sweet smell of sick old man came through the air to my cringing nostrils. I did not want to breathe the air he breathed. As my mother might have said about something I'd picked up in the street, I did not know where that air might have been. It might still have had bits in it from the trenches of the Great War, where dead men hung rotting on the barbed wire. Particles of poison gas; or the dying breath breathed out by the dead Austrian ...

In the soft glow of the gas-mantle,[8] his face was all

[8] gauze around a gas-jet

wrinkled and shadowed pits, mysterious as craters of the moon. He was fiddling with the tap of the gas-light, fixing a little bit of wire round it. Perhaps it was his way of keeping me at bay, as my comics were my way of keeping him at bay.

He had dragged out of some cupboard a large old stained tea-chest. It was full of strange shapes, trapped in tangled coils of wire. The strange shapes drew me irresistibly; perhaps I had some wild hope of building another jangle-machine. I put a tentative hand inside. There was the most huge rusty hammer I'd ever seen ... a long weird knife in a scabbard.[9] I tugged at the knife; it resisted. I tugged harder ... then harder. It leapt out of my hand, dragging behind it, in a web of tangled wire, a queerly shaped, huge brass tap, and a short brass cylinder. They all fell on the floor with a terrible bang. He swung round, ever-jumpy ...

I gabbled out, before he could hit me,

'What's that funny tap, Granda?'

He picked up the tap, as if he hadn't seen it in a long time.

'By,' he said dreamily, 'that's a spare tap left over from the old *Mauretania*. Finest and fastest ship in the world, she was. Held the Blue Riband of the Atlantic for twenty years. The day she was launched – she had no funnels or nothing, mind – the shipyard workers got up steam in a little donkey-boiler in the bows. The old Morrie was the only liner ever launched wi' steam up. And when she sailed on her maiden voyage, people lined the banks of the Tyne for eight miles to bid her Godspeed. As if the King was passin' ... and when she came home from her last voyage, to be broken up to make razor blades, the people lined up again to say

[9] case or sheath that protects a blade

goodbye to her. Look, here's the pictures.' And there, on the wall, were two photographs of the old Morrie sailing and the old Morrie coming home. And she looked the same in both.

'Why did they break her up? She looks as good as new.'

'Aye, but she was tired *inside,*' he said. 'Things look the same, but they get tired inside.' There was something in his voice I couldn't face. So I held up the short brass cylinder before the silence came back like the frozen Arctic.

'That's the lens of the film-projector that showed the first movie ever shown in North Shields. The show was held in the Temperance Hall, and it cost a penny to get in. Fatty Arbuckle was the star – he got sent to prison in the end. We saw Charlie Chaplin through that. Rudolph Valentino. No talkies of course – just a lady playing the piano for the exciting bits.'

'How did you get it?'

'George Costigan gave it to me in Guthrie's Bar, the night the old King died . . .'

'And what's this?' I held up a worn long block of rubber.

'That's the brake-block off me old bike – the one I used to ride round Holywell Dene, when I was courting your nana. I was taking that brake-block off, the night your dad was born . . .' A new kind of awe swept over me. My mother had often talked about the night *I* was born (and what a hard time I'd given her, and how she'd almost died of me), and that was mysterious enough. But the night my *dad* was born . . . that was as incredibly far off as the Pharaohs building the pyramids.

We were off in style now. Every object told a story. The dead rose up and walked again. Admiral Jellicoe and Earl Kitchener of Khartoum. Kaiser Bill and Marie Lloyd. Lloyd George and Jack the Ripper. They streamed out of my grandfather as they might have streamed out of the first cinema-projector to show a film in North Shields.

Only once was he silent. About the long knife in the scabbard. He took it in his hand and was silent, then he put it back in the box. I knew it was the bayonet that had killed the Austrian, for his face went grey, and his eyes were far away. I knew he hated it. I also knew he would never throw it away. Just like the cap-badge.

'What did you do in the trenches – in between?' I asked.

'I'll tell yer.' He pulled out a steel helmet, thick with rust. 'See that little hole in the top?'

'Is it a bullet-hole?'

He actually laughed. 'No, no. It's a screw-hole. We used to pull the screw out and stick a nail through the hole, and stick a candle on the nail. So we could see to play cards. Look – you can still see a bit o' candle-grease. I was good at cards – three-card brag, a quick game – it didn't matter if you were interrupted, like. I won a lot o' money. Lot o' fellers still owe me money, but they're dead. So I took a little thing from their kit, instead. To remember them by. See ...' He reached up and took down his shaving-tackle from above the sink.

'That's Gerry Henry's shaving brush, and Mannie Webber's bowl, and Tommy Malbon's mirror ... Good chums, every one.'

Now we were both silent, and it was all right. For I knew who was in the silence now. The good chums, every one.

It was Granda who broke the silence. 'There was a joke as we used to have, us Shields lads out there:

The boy stood on the burning deck,
His feet were full o' blisters.
His father stood in Guthrie's Bar
Wi' the beer running down his whiskers.

We always said that, when we were down. It always got a laugh.'

He laughed. I laughed. It seemed good to laugh with good chums.

When my parents got back from the hospital, it was over for that night. I was reverently arranging objects in sections and patterns across the clippie rug, and Granda was peacefully snoring in his chair.

But he'd done enough. Taught me that every object tells a story, and every dent in every object tells a story. Within a week I was pressing my nose against the window of every junk-shop in town. Regarding the scruffy little men who stood inside, rubbing their hands together against the cold, as the Lords of Time who knew all mysteries.

After that, museums. Like the museum I sit in now.

Then, it was a dent in a tap made thirty years ago. Now it is a dent in a Pharaoh's head made four thousand years ago. All part of my journey back in time. The world goes forward to drugs and violence and fruit-machine addiction. I go backwards, to where I am truly free.

My grandfather, long gone where old soldiers go, still accompanies me. His photograph is on my desk as I write; his photo before the gas got him, on the Somme. When my nana married him, she said he was the handsomest feller in Shields, with his bonnie blue eyes ... He is much younger in his photo than I am now.

Each year I look more like him, as I remember him:

the incredibly bushy eyebrows; the hairs that persist in growing on the end of my nose. When I laugh, I hear the echo of his laugh. Sometimes I hear myself wheezing in the mornings, though I was never gassed at the Battle of the Somme.

Time moves; in all directions. My grandfather made me.

The Coup de Grâce

by Ambrose Bierce

The fighting had been hard and continuous; that was attested by all the senses. The very taste of battle was in the air. All was now over; it remained only to succour[1] the wounded and bury the dead – to 'tidy up a bit', as the humorist of a burial squad put it. A good deal of 'tidying up' was required. As far as one could see through the forests, among the splintered trees, lay wrecks of men and horses. Among them moved the stretcher-bearers, gathering and carrying away the few who showed signs of life. Most of the wounded had died of neglect while the right to minister to their wants was in dispute. It is an army regulation that the wounded must wait, the best way to care for them is to win the battle. It must be confessed that victory is a distinct advantage to a man requiring attention, but many do not live to avail themselves of it.

The dead were collected in groups of a dozen or a score and laid side by side in rows while the trenches were dug to receive them. Some, found at too great a distance from these rallying points, were buried where they lay. There was little attempt at identification, though in most cases, the burial parties being detailed to glean[2] the same ground which they had assisted to reap, the names of the victorious dead were known and

[1] help in distress
[2] a harvest image – to gather the corn left by the reapers

listed. The enemy's fallen had to be content with counting. But of that they got enough: many of them were counted several times, and the total, as given afterward in the official report of the victorious commander, denoted rather a hope than a result.

At some little distance from the spot where one of the burial parties had established its 'bivouac[3] of the dead', a man in the uniform of a Federal officer[4] stood leaning against a tree. From his feet upward to his neck his attitude was that of weariness reposing; but he turned his head uneasily from side to side; his mind was apparently not at rest. He was perhaps uncertain in which direction to go; he was not likely to remain long where he was, for already the level rays of the setting sun straggled redly through the open spaces of the wood and the weary soldiers were quitting their task for the day. He would hardly make a night of it alone there among the dead. Nine men in ten whom you meet after a battle inquire the way to some fraction of the army – as if any one could know. Doubtless this officer was lost. After resting himself a moment he would presumably follow one of the retiring burial squads.

When all were gone he walked straight away into the forest toward the red west, its light staining his face like blood. The air of confidence with which he now strode along showed that he was on familiar ground; he had recovered his bearings. The dead on his right and on his left were unregarded as he passed. An occasional low moan from some sorely stricken wretch whom the relief-parties had not reached, and who would have to pass a comfortless night beneath the stars with his thirst to keep him company, was equally unheeded. What,

[3] temporary camp in the open air
[4] a soldier of the US government in the Civil War (1861–5)

indeed, could the officer have done, being no surgeon and having no water?

At the head of a shallow ravine, a mere depression of the ground, lay a small group of bodies. He saw, and swerving suddenly from his course walked rapidly toward them. Scanning each one sharply as he passed, he stopped at last above one which lay at a slight remove from the others, near a clump of small trees. He looked at it narrowly. It seemed to stir. He stooped and laid his hand upon its face. It screamed.

The officer was Captain Downing Madwell, of a Massachusetts regiment of infantry, a daring and intelligent soldier, an honourable man.

In the regiment were two brothers named Halcrow – Caffal and Creede Halcrow. Caffal Halcrow was a sergeant in Captain Madwell's company, and these two men, the sergeant and the captain, were devoted friends. In so far as disparity of rank, difference in duties and considerations of military discipline would permit they were commonly together. They had, indeed, grown up together from childhood. A habit of the heart is not easily broken off. Caffal Halcrow had nothing military in his taste nor disposition, but the thought of separation from his friend was disagreeable; he enlisted in the company in which Madwell was second-lieutenant. Each had taken two steps upward in rank, but between the highest non-commissioned and the lowest commissioned officer the gulf is deep and wide and the old relation was maintained with difficulty and a difference.

Creede Halcrow, the brother of Caffal, was the major of the regiment – a cynical, saturnine[5] man, between whom and Captain Madwell there was a natural

[5] gloomy character or appearance

antipathy which circumstances had nourished and strengthened to an active animosity. But for the restraining influence of their mutual relation to Caffal these two patriots would doubtless have endeavoured to deprive their country of each other's services.

At the opening of the battle that morning the regiment was performing outpost duty a mile away from the main army. It was attacked and nearly surrounded in the forest, but stubbornly held its ground. During a lull in the fighting, Major Halcrow came to Captain Madwell. The two exchanged formal salutes, and the major said: 'Captain, the colonel directs that you push your company to the head of this ravine and hold your place there until recalled. I need hardly apprise you of the dangerous character of the movement, but if you wish, you can, I suppose, turn over the command to your first-lieutenant. I was not, however, directed to authorise the substitution; it is merely a suggestion of my own, unofficially made.'

To this deadly insult Captain Madwell coolly replied:

'Sir, I invite you to accompany the movement. A mounted officer would be a conspicuous mark, and I have long held the opinion that it would be better if you were dead.'

The art of repartee[6] was cultivated in military circles as early as 1862.

A half-hour later Captain Madwell's company was driven from its position at the head of the ravine, with a loss of one-third its number. Among the fallen was Sergeant Halcrow. The regiment was soon afterward forced back to the main line, and at the close of the battle was miles away. The captain was now standing at the side of his subordinate and friend.

[6] witty exchange of words

Sergeant Halcrow was mortally hurt. His clothing was deranged; it seemed to have been violently torn apart, exposing the abdomen. Some of the buttons of his jacket had been pulled off and lay on the ground beside him and fragments of his other garments were strewn about. His leather belt was parted and had apparently been dragged from beneath him as he lay. There had been no great effusion of blood. The only visible wound was a wide, ragged opening in the abdomen. It was defiled with earth and dead leaves. Protruding from it was a loop of small intestine. In all his experience Captain Madwell had not seen a wound like this. He could neither conjecture how it was made nor explain the attendant circumstances – the strangely torn clothing, the parted belt, the besmirching of the white skin. He knelt and made a closer examination. When he rose to his feet, he turned his eyes in different directions as if looking for an enemy. Fifty yards away, on the crest of a low, thinly wooded hill, he saw several dark objects moving about among the fallen men – a herd of swine. One stood with its back to him, its shoulders sharply elevated. Its forefeet were upon a human body, its head was depressed and invisible. The bristly ridge of its chine[7] showed black against the red west. Captain Madwell drew away his eyes and fixed them again upon the thing which had been his friend.

The man who had suffered these monstrous mutilations was alive. At intervals he moved his limbs; he moaned at every breath. He stared blankly into the face of his friend and if touched screamed. In his giant agony he had torn up the ground on which he lay; his clenched hands were full of leaves and twigs and earth. Articulate speech was beyond his power; it was impos-

[7] backbone

sible to know if he were sensible to anything but pain. The expression of his face was an appeal; his eyes were full of prayer. For what?

There was no misreading that look; the captain had too frequently seen it in eyes of those whose lips had still the power to formulate it by an entreaty for death. Consciously or unconsciously, this writhing fragment of humanity, this type and example of acute sensation, this handiwork of man and beast, this humble, unheroic Prometheus,[8] was imploring everything, all, the whole non-ego, for the boon of oblivion. To the earth and the sky alike, to the trees, to the man, to whatever took form in sense or consciousness, this incarnate suffering addressed that silent plea.

For what, indeed? For that which we accord to even the meanest creature without sense to demand it, denying it only to the wretched of our own race; for the blessed release, the rite of uttermost compassion, the *coup de grâce.*[9]

Captain Madwell spoke the name of his friend. He repeated it over and over without effect until emotion choked his utterance. His tears plashed upon the livid face beneath his own and blinded himself. He saw nothing but a blurred and moving object, but the moans were more distinct than ever, interrupted at briefer intervals by sharper shrieks. He turned away, struck his hand upon his forehead, and strode from the spot. The swine, catching sight of him, threw up their crimson muzzles, regarding him suspiciously a second, and then with a gruff, concerted grunt, raced away out

[8] in Greek mythology Prometheus stole fire from heaven to help human kind and was punished by being chained to a rock. An eagle tore out his liver every day.

[9] French for 'stroke of mercy' – a blow or shot that brings death to someone suffering

of sight. A horse, its foreleg splintered by a cannon-shot, lifted its head sidewise from the ground and neighed piteously. Madwell stepped forward, drew his revolver and shot the poor beast between the eyes, narrowly observing its death-struggle, which, contrary to his expectation, was violent and long; but at last it lay still. The tense muscles of its lips, which had uncovered the teeth in a horrible grin, relaxed; the sharp, clean-cut profile took on a look of profound peace and rest.

Along the distant, thinly wooded crest to westward the fringe of sunset fire had now nearly burned itself out. The light upon the trunks of the trees had faded to a tender grey; shadows were in their tops, like great dark birds aperch. Night was coming and there were miles of haunted forest between Captain Madwell and camp. Yet he stood there at the side of the dead animal, apparently lost to all sense of his surroundings. His eyes were bent upon the earth at his feet; his left hand hung loosely at his side, his right still held the pistol. Presently he lifted his face, turned it toward his dying friend and walked rapidly back to his side. He knelt upon one knee, cocked the weapon, placed the muzzle against the man's forehead, and turning away his eyes pulled the trigger. There was no report. He had used his last cartridge for the horse.

The sufferer moaned and his lips moved convulsively. The froth that ran from them had a tinge of blood.

Captain Madwell rose to his feet and drew his sword from the scabbard. He passed the fingers of his left hand along the edge from hilt to point. He held it out straight before him, as if to test his nerves. There was no visible tremor of the blade; the ray of bleak skylight that it reflected was steady and true. He stooped and with his left hand tore away the dying man's shirt, rose and placed the point of the sword just over the heart.

This time he did not withdraw his eyes. Grasping the hilt with both hands, he thrust downward with all his strength and weight. The blade sank into the man's body – through his body into the earth; Captain Madwell came near falling forward upon his work. The dying man drew up his knees and at the same time threw his right arm across his breast and grasped the steel so tightly that the knuckles of the hand visibly whitened. By a violent but vain effort to withdraw the blade the wound was enlarged; a rill of blood escaped, running sinuously down into the deranged clothing. At that moment three men stepped silently forward from behind the clump of young trees which had concealed their approach. Two were hospital attendants and carried a stretcher.

The third was Major Creede Halcrow.

Two Friends

by Guy de Maupassant
translated by Roger Colet

Scenes Maupassant witnessed as a young private in the French army in 1870 played a strong part in his stories. The French emperor Napoleon III declared war on Prussia in July 1870, on learning that a German was a candidate for the Spanish throne. (Prussia was a kingdom in northern Germany.) In September 1870 the French army was defeated by the Prussians, Napoleon was captured and France became a Republic. The Prussians besieged Paris from September 1870 until January 1871, intending to starve it into surrender.

Paris was under siege, starving and at her last gasp. The sparrows were disappearing from the roofs, and the city's sewers were being depopulated. People were eating anything they could find.

One bright morning in January Monsieur Morissot, a watchmaker by trade but an idler by necessity, was walking sadly along the outer boulevard[1] with an empty stomach and his hands in the pockets of his uniform trousers when he came face to face with a comrade in arms whom he recognised as an old friend. It was Monsieur Sauvage, a riverside acquaintance.

Every Sunday before the war Morissot used to leave home at dawn with a bamboo rod in his hand and a tin box on his back. He took the Argenteuil train, got out at Colombes, and walked to Marante Island. As soon as

[1] wide road

he reached this place of his dreams he started fishing and he went on fishing till nightfall.

There, every Sunday, he used to meet another fanatical angler, a stout, jolly little man called Monsieur Sauvage, a haberdasher[2] from the Rue Notre-Dame-de-Lorette. They often spent half the day sitting side by side with their rods in their hands and their feet dangling over the water; and they had become firm friends.

Some days they never said a word; sometimes they chatted. But they understood each other perfectly without any need for words, having similar tastes and identical feelings.

On spring mornings, about ten o'clock, when a faint mist was rising from the smooth surface of the river and drifting along with the current, and the two enthusiastic anglers could feel the pleasant warmth of the spring sun on their backs, Morissot would say to his neighbour: 'This is the life, eh?'

And Monsieur Sauvage would reply: 'This is the life all right.'

That was all that was necessary for them to understand and respect one another.

In the autumn, towards the end of the day, when the setting sun reddened the sky and stained the river crimson, when the horizon was ablaze and the water reflected the shapes of scarlet clouds, and when the trees between the two friends, already russet-coloured and shivering with the foretaste of winter, turned fiery red and gold, Monsieur Sauvage would look at Morissot with a smile and say: 'What a picture!'

And Morissot, struck by the beauty of the scene but keeping his eyes fixed on his float, would reply: 'Better than the boulevard, isn't it?'

[2] seller of sewing or dressmaking materials, gloves, hats, and so on

They had no sooner recognised each other than they shook hands warmly, struck by the changed circumstances in which they had met. Monsieur Sauvage heaved a sigh and murmured: 'What a mess we're in!'

Morissot answered gloomily: 'And what weather we're having! This is the first fine day we've had this year.'

The sky was indeed a bright unclouded blue.

They walked on together, side by side, sad and thoughtful.

'Remember our fishing?' Morissot went on. 'Those were the days!'

'I wonder when we'll go fishing again,' said Monsieur Sauvage.

They went into a little café and had an absinthe[3] together. Then they resumed their stroll along the pavement.

Suddenly Morissot stopped short.

'What about another?'

'I won't say no,' replied Monsieur Sauvage, and they went into another café.

When they came out they were rather fuddled, as people are when they have been drinking spirits on an empty stomach. It was a mild day and a gentle breeze fanned their faces.

The warm air made Monsieur Sauvage, already intoxicated by the absinthe, quite tipsy. He stopped and said: 'Let's go.'

'Where?'

'Fishing of course.'

'But where?'

'Why, our usual island. The French outposts aren't far from Colombes. I know Colonel Dumoulin: they'll let us through without any trouble.'

[3] strong aniseed-flavoured liqueur

Quivering with excitement, Morissot replied: 'Right, I'm with you.'

And they separated to go and get their fishing tackle.

An hour later they were walking side by side along the main road. Eventually they reached the villa which the colonel was using as his headquarters. He smiled at their whimsical request and gave his consent. They set off again, armed with a pass.

Before long they had crossed the line of outposts, passed through the deserted village of Colombes, and found themselves on the edge of the little vineyards which sloped down to the Seine. It was about eleven o'clock.

Across the river, the village of Argenteuil looked dead. The heights of Orgemont and Sannois dominated the whole countryside. The great plain which stretches as far as Nanterre was empty, completely empty, with its bare cherry trees and its grey fields.

Pointing to the high ground, Monsieur Sauvage murmured: 'The Prussians are up there.'

And a paralysing sense of anxiety took hold of the two friends as they looked at this deserted scene.

The Prussians! They had never seen any of them, but for months they had been aware of their presence around Paris, bringing ruin on France, looting, murdering, starving, invisible and irresistible. And a sort of superstitious terror was added to the hatred they felt for that unknown, victorious people.

'Suppose we met some of them,' stammered Morissot, 'what would we do?'

With that mocking Parisian humour which had survived in spite of everything, Monsieur Sauvage replied: 'We'd offer them some fish to fry.'

But they hesitated about venturing into the open country, intimidated by the silence all around them.

At last Monsieur Sauvage made up his mind.

'Come on, let's go,' he said, 'but keep your eyes skinned!'

And they went down into a vineyard, bent double or crawling along, their ears cocked and their eyes darting about nervously.

They still had a strip of open ground to cross to reach the river bank. They broke into a run, and as soon as they got to the bank they crouched down among the dry rushes.

Morissot put his ear to the ground to listen for the sound of footsteps in their vicinity. He heard nothing. They were alone, absolutely alone.

Feeling reassured, they started to fish.

In front of them Marante Island, now deserted, hid them from the opposite bank. The little restaurant was closed and looked as if it had been abandoned for years.

Monsieur Sauvage caught the first gudgeon,[4] Morissot the second, and after that they kept lifting their rods every other moment with little silver creatures wriggling at the end of the lines – a miraculous draught of fishes!

They carefully slipped the fish into a fine-meshed net bag dangling in the water at their feet, and a feeling of joy took hold of them, that delicious joy one feels at rediscovering a pleasure after being deprived of it for months.

The kindly sun warmed their backs; they heard nothing and thought of nothing; the rest of the world no longer existed for them; they simply fished.

But suddenly a dull roar which seemed to come from under the ground made the earth tremble. The big guns were opening up again.

[4] a small fresh-water fish

Morissot turned his head, and above the bank, away to the left, he saw the great bulk of Mont-Valérien, its summit sporting a white plume, a puff of smoke it had just spat out.

The next moment a second puff of smoke came from the top of the fort, and a few seconds later the boom of another detonation reached their ears.

Others followed, as in quick succession the hill sent out its deadly breath, emitting clouds of milky vapour which rose slowly into the peaceful sky to form a cloud above the fort.

Monsieur Sauvage shrugged his shoulders.

'There they go, at it again!' he said.

Morissot, who was anxiously watching the feather on his float bobbing up and down, was suddenly filled with a peace-loving man's anger at these madmen who insisted on fighting one another, and he growled: 'They must be fools, killing each other like that.'

'They're worse than wild beasts,' said Monsieur Sauvage.

And Morissot, who had just hooked a bleak,[5] declared: 'To think that it'll always be like that as long as we have governments!'

Monsieur Sauvage corrected him: 'The Republic would never have declared war ...'

'With kings,' Morissot broke in, 'you have war abroad; with republics, you have war at home.'

They started a friendly argument, discussing the great political problems with the sweet reasonableness of peaceful men of limited intelligence, and agreeing on one point: that men would never be free. And all the time Mont-Valérien went on thundering, destroying French houses with its shells, pulverising human lives,

[5] a small river-fish

crushing bodies, putting an end to countless dreams, countless expectations, countless hopes of happiness, and inflicting wounds that would never heal on the hearts of girls, wives and mothers in other lands.

'Such is life,' said Monsieur Sauvage.

'Or rather, such is death,' retorted Morissot with a laugh.

Then they gave a start of terror as they became aware that somebody was moving behind them. Looking round they saw four armed men standing right behind them – four big, bearded men, dressed like liveried servants with flat caps on their heads, covering them with rifles.

The two rods dropped from their hands and floated away down the river.

In a matter of seconds they were seized, bound, marched off, thrown into a boat, and ferried across to the island.

Behind the house they had thought to be deserted they saw a score of German soldiers.

A hairy giant of a man, sitting astride a chair and smoking a large porcelain pipe, asked them in excellent French: 'Well, gentlemen, have you had a good day's fishing?'

Just then one of the soldiers deposited at his feet the net bag full of fish, which he had taken care to bring along.

The Prussian officer smiled: 'Ah, I see you weren't doing so badly. But that's not what I want to talk to you about. Listen to me and don't get alarmed.

'As far as I'm concerned, you are a couple of spies sent to keep an eye on me. I capture you and shoot you. You pretend to be fishing to conceal your real intentions. You have fallen into my hands: so much the worse for you. War is war.

'But as you came out here through your own lines, I presume you have a password in order to get back. Give me that password and I'll spare your lives.'

The two friends were standing side by side, ashen-faced. Their hands were trembling slightly, but they said nothing.

The officer went on: 'Nobody will be any the wiser. You will go back as if nothing had happened, and the secret will go with you. If you refuse, you die – you die on the spot. Now choose.'

They remained motionless and made no reply.

The Prussian pointed to the water and calmly continued: 'Five minutes from now you will be at the bottom of that river. Five minutes! You've got relatives waiting for you, I presume?'

Mont-Valérien was still firing.

The two anglers stood there silent. The German gave an order in his own language. Then he moved his chair so as not to be too close to the prisoners; and twelve men took up a position at a distance of twenty paces, their rifles at the order.

'I give you one minute,' said the officer, 'not a second more.'

Then he suddenly got to his feet, went over to the two Frenchmen, took Morissot by the arm, and led him to one side.

'Quick, the password,' he whispered. 'Your friend will never know. I'll pretend I've relented.'

Morissot made no reply.

The Prussian then took Monsieur Sauvage aside and made the same suggestion to him.

Monsieur Sauvage said nothing.

They found themselves together again, side by side.

The officer gave an order. The soldiers raised their rifles.

Just then Morissot's eye fell on the net bag full of gudgeon lying on the grass a few feet away. The pile of fish, which were still wriggling, glistened in a ray of sunshine. He felt a momentary weakness. Try as he might to hold them back, tears came into his eyes.

'Good-bye, Monsieur Sauvage,' he stammered.

'Good-bye, Monsieur Morissot,' said his friend.

They shook hands, trembling uncontrollably from head to foot.

'Fire!' shouted the officer.

The twelve shots rang out together.

Monsieur Sauvage fell forward like a log. Morissot, being taller, swayed, spun round, and fell across his friend's body. He lay there with his face to the sky while blood gushed out of the holes in the front of his tunic.

The German gave another order.

His men dispersed and came back with some lengths of rope and some stones which they fastened to the feet of the two dead men; then they carried them to the bank.

Mont-Valérien was firing all the time, capped now by a huge cloud of smoke.

Two soldiers took Morissot by the head and feet. Two others picked up Monsieur Sauvage in the same way. They swung them backwards and forwards and threw them as far as they could. The bodies described a curve in the air, then, weighted by the stones, plunged feet-first into the river.

The water splashed, bubbled and quivered, then became calm again. A few tiny waves spread to each bank.

A little blood was floating on the surface.

Still perfectly calm, the officer murmured to himself: 'Now it's the fishes' turn.'

And he set off back to the house.

Suddenly he noticed the bag of gudgeon on the grass. He picked it up, examined it, smiled, and shouted: 'Wilhelm!'

A soldier in a white apron came running up. Throwing him the two dead men's haul, the officer said: 'Fry these little things for me straight away while they are still alive. They'll be delicious.'

Then he lit his pipe again.

Pigeons

by Michael McLaverty

After years of unrest, in 1921 Ireland was divided politically into the twenty-six counties of the Irish Free State, and the six counties of Northern Ireland, which is part of the United Kingdom. A civil war followed, then in 1937 the Irish Republic's links with England were ended and it became known as Eire. The flag used to represent Eire is green, white and gold. In the story, the policeman removes it from the coffin to show his support for England. The harp is an old symbol for Ireland and was used on a flag displayed by English sovereigns; so the badge of harp and crown worn by the policemen shows their belief that Ireland should be under the rule of England. The main religion of the Republic is Roman Catholic; in Northern Ireland Protestants are in the majority. The family in the story are Roman Catholics.

Our Johnny kept pigeons, three white ones and a brown one that could tumble in the air like a leaf. They were nice pigeons, but they dirtied the slates and cooed so early in the morning that my daddy said that some day he would wring their bloody necks. That is a long while ago now, for we still have the pigeons, but Johnny is dead; he died for Ireland.

Whenever I think of our Johnny I always think of Saturday. Nearly every Saturday night he had something for me, maybe sweets, a toy train, a whistle, or glass marbles with rainbows inside them. I would be in bed when he'd come home; I always tried to keep awake, but my eyes wouldn't let me – they always closed tight when I wasn't thinking. We both slept together in the wee back room, and when Johnny came up to bed he always lit the gas, the gas that had no mantle. If he had something for me he would shake me and say; 'Frankie, Frankie, are you asleep?' My eyes would be very gluey and I would rub them with my fists until they would open in the gaslight. For a long while I would see gold needles sticking out of the flame, then they would melt away and the gas become like a pansy leaf with a blue heart. Johnny would be standing beside the bed and I would smile all blinky[1] at him. Maybe he'd stick a sweet in my mouth, but if I hadn't said my prayers he'd lift me out onto the cold, cold floor. When I would be jumping in again in my shirt-tails, he would play whack at me and laugh if he got me. Soon he would climb into bed and tell me about the ice-cream shops, and the bird shop that had funny pigeons and rabbits and mice in the window. Some day he was going to bring me down the town and buy me a black and white mouse, and a custard bun full of ice cream. But he'll never do it now because he died for Ireland.

On Saturdays, too, I watched for him at the back door when he was coming from work. He always came over the waste ground, because it was the shortest. His dungarees would be all shiny, but they hadn't a nice smell. I would pull them off him, and he would lift me onto his shoulder, and swing me round and round until my head got light and the things in the kitchen went up and down. My mammie said he had me spoilt. He always gave me pennies on Saturday, two pennies, and I bought a liquorice pipe with one penny and kept the other for Sunday. Then he would go into the cold

[1] because of his gluey eyes, blinking frequently

scullery[2] to wash his black hands and face; he would stand at the sink, scrubbing and scrubbing and singing 'The Old Rusty Bridge by the Mill', but if you went near him he'd squirt soap in your eye. After he had washed himself, we would get our Saturday dinner, the dinner with the sausages because it was payday. Johnny used to give me a bit of his sausages, but if my mammie saw me she'd slap me for taking the bite out of his mouth. It was a long, long wait before we went out to the yard to the pigeons.

The pigeon shed was on the slates above the closet. There was a ladder up to it, but Johnny wouldn't let me climb for fear I'd break my neck. But I used to climb up when he wasn't looking. There was a great flutter and flapping of wings when Johnny would open the trap door to let them out. They would fly out in a line, brownie first and the white ones last. We would lie on the waste ground at the back of our street watching them fly. They would fly round and round, rising higher and higher each time. Then they would fly so high we would blink our eyes and lose them in the blue sky. But Johnny always found them first. 'I can see them, Frankie,' he would say. 'Yonder they are. Look! Above the brickyard chimney.' He would put his arm around my neck, pointing with his outstretched hand. I would strain my eyes, and at last I would see them, their wings flashing in the sun as they turned towards home. They were great flyers. But brownie would get tired and he would tumble head over heels like you'd think he was going to fall. The white ones always flew down to him, and Johnny would go wild. 'He's a good tumbler, but he won't let the others fly high. I think I'll sell him.' He would look at me, plucking at the grass, afraid to look

[2] small room where washing-up and other kitchen work is done

up. 'Ah, Frankie,' he would say, 'I won't sell him. Sure I'm only codding.'[3] All day we would sit if the weather was good, watching our pigeons flying, and brownie doing somersaults. When they were tired they would light on the blue slates, and Johnny would throw corn up to them. Saturday was a great day for us and for our pigeons, but it was on Saturday that Johnny died for Ireland.

We were lying, as usual, at the back, while the pigeons were let out for a fly round. It was a lovely sunny day. Every house had clothes out on the lines, and the clothes were fluttering in the breeze. Some of the neighbours were sitting at their back doors, nursing babies or darning socks. They weren't nice neighbours for they told the rent man about the shed on the slates, and he made us pay a penny a week for it. But we didn't talk much to them, for we loved our pigeons, and on that lovely day we were splitting our sides laughing at the way brownie was tumbling, when a strange man in a black hat and Burberry coat came near us. Johnny jumped up and went to meet him. I saw them talking, with their heads bent towards the ground, and then the strange man went away. Johnny looked very sad and he didn't laugh at brownie any more. He gave me the things out of his pockets, a penknife, a key and a little blue notebook with its edges all curled. 'Don't say anything to Mammie. Look after the pigeons, Frankie, until I come back. I won't be long.' He gave my hand a tight squeeze, then he walked away without turning round to wave at me.

All that day I lay out watching the pigeons, and when I got tired I opened the notebook. It had a smell of fags and there was fag dust inside it. I could read what he had written down:

[3] joking

Corn	2s. 6d.
Club	6d.
3 Pkts. Woodbine[4]	6d.
Frankie	2d.

He had the same thing written down on a whole lot of pages; if he had been at school he would have got slapped for wasting the good paper. I put the notebook in my pocket when my mammie called me for my tea. She asked me about Johnny and I told her he wouldn't be long until he was back. Then it got late. The pigeons flew off the slates and into the shed, and still Johnny didn't come back.

It came on night. My sisters were sent out to look for him. My daddy came home from work. We were all in now, my two sisters and Mammie and Daddy, everyone except Johnny. Daddy took out his pipe with the tin lid but he didn't light it. We were all quiet, but my mother's hands would move from her lap to her chin, and she was sighing. The kettle began humming and shuffling the lid about, and my daddy lifted it off the fire and placed it on the warm hob. The clock on the mantelpiece chimed eleven and my sisters blessed themselves – it got a soul out of purgatory[5] when you did that. They forgot all about my bedtime and I was let stay up though my eyes felt full of sand. The rain was falling. We could hear it slapping in the yard and trindling down the grate. It was a blowy night for someone's back door was banging, making the dogs bark. The newspapers that lay on the scullery floor to keep it clean began to crackle up and down with the wind till you'd have thought there was a mouse under

[4] a brand of cigarette ('fags')

[5] Roman Catholic Christians are taught that this is a place of punishment after death.

them. A bicycle bell rang in the street outside our kitchen window and it made Mammie jump. Then a motor rattled down, shaking the house and the vases on the shelf. My daddy opened the scullery door and went into the yard. The gas blinked and a coughing smell of a chimney burning came into the kitchen. I'm sure it was Mrs Ryan's. She always burnt hers on a wet night. If the peelers[6] caught her she'd be locked in jail, for you weren't allowed to burn your own chimney.

I wished Daddy would burn ours. It was nice to see him putting the bunch of lighted papers on the yard brush and sticking them up the wide chimney. The chimney would roar, and if you went outside you'd see lines of sparks like hot wires coming out and the smoke bubbling over like lemonade in a bottle. But he wouldn't burn it tonight, because we were waiting on Johnny.

'Is there any sign of him?' said Mammie, when Daddy came in again.

'None yet; but he'll be all right; he'll be all right. We'll say the prayers, and he'll be in before we're finished.'

We were just ready to kneel when a knock came to the back door. It was a very dim knock and we all sat still, listening. 'That's him now,' said Daddy, and I saw my mother's face brightening. Daddy went into the yard and I heard the stiff bar on the door opening and feet shuffling. 'Easy now: easy now,' said someone. Then Daddy came in, his face as white as a sheet. He said something to Mammie. 'Mother of God it isn't true – it isn't!' she said. Daddy turned and sent me up to bed.

Up in the wee room I could see down into the yard. The light from the kitchen shone into it and I saw men with black hats and the rain falling on them like little

[6] policeman

needles, but I couldn't see Johnny. I looked up at the shed on the slates, the rain was melting down its sides, and the wet felt was shining like new boots. When I looked into the yard again, Daddy was bending over something. I got frightened and went into my sisters' room. They were crying and I cried too, while I sat shivering in my shirt and my teeth chattering. 'What's wrong?' I asked. But they only cried and said: 'Nothing, son. Nothing. Go to sleep, Frankie, like a good little boy.' My big sister put me into her bed, and put the clothes around me and stroked my head. Then she lay on the top of the bed beside me, and I could feel her breathing heavily on my back. Outside it was still blowy for the wind was kicking an empty salmon tin which rattled along the street. For a long time I listened to the noises the wind made, and then I slept.

In the morning when I opened my eyes I wondered at finding myself in my sisters' room. It was very still: the blinds were down and the room was full of yellow light. I listened for the sound of plates, a brush scrubbing, or my big sister singing. But I heard nothing, neither inside the house nor outside it. I remembered about last night, my sisters crying because our Johnny didn't come home. I sat up in bed; I felt afraid because the house was strange, and I got out and went into the wee back room.

The door was open and there was yellow light in it, too, and the back of the bed had white cloth and I couldn't see over it. Then I saw my mammie in the room, sitting on a chair. She stretched out her arms and I ran across and knelt beside her, burying my face in her lap. She had on a smooth, black dress, and I could smell the camphor[7] balls off it, the smell that kills the moths, the funny things with no blood and no bones

[7] a substance used in mothballs

that eat holes in your jersey. There were no holes in Mammie's dress. She rubbed my head with her hands and said: 'You're the only boy I have now.' I could hear her heart thumping very hard, and then she cried, and I cried and cried, with my head down on her lap. 'What's wrong, Mammie?' I asked, looking up at her wet eyes. 'Nothing, darling: nothing, pet. He died for Ireland.' I turned my head and looked at the bed. Johnny was lying on the white bed in a brown dress. His hands were pale and they were joined around his rosary beads,[8] and a big crucifix between them. There was a big lump of wadding at the side of his head and wee pieces up his nose. I cried more and more, and then my mammie made me put on my clothes, and go downstairs for my breakfast.

All that day my mammie stayed in the room to talk to the people that came to see our Johnny. And all the women shook hands with Mammie and they all said the same thing: 'I'm sorry for your trouble, but he died for his country.' They knelt beside the white bed and prayed, and then sat for a while looking at Johnny, and speaking in low whispers. My sisters brought them wine and biscuits, and some of them cried when they were taking it, dabbing their eyes with their handkerchiefs or the tails of their shawls. Mrs McCann came and she got wine, too, though she had told the rent man about the shed on the slates and we had to pay a penny a week. I was in the wee room when she came, and I saw her looking at the lighted candles and the flowers on the table, and up at the gas that had no mantle. But she couldn't see it because my big sister had put white paper over it, and she had done the same with the four brass knobs on the bed. She began to sniff and sniff and

[8] a string of beads that help a Catholic Christian to pray

my mammie opened the window without saying anything. The blind began to snuffle in and out, the lighted candles to waggle, and the flowers to smell. We could hear the pigeons cooing and flapping on the shed, and I could see at the back of my eyes their necks fattening and their feathers bristling like a dog going to fight. It's well Daddy didn't hear them or he might have wrung their necks.

At night the kitchen was crammed with men and women, and many had to sit in the cold scullery. Mrs Ryan, next door, lent us her chairs for the people to sit on. There was lemonade and biscuits and tea and porter. Some of the men, who drank black porter, gave me pennies, and they smoked and talked all night. The kitchen was full of smoke and it made your eyes sting. One man told my daddy he should be a proud man, because Johnny had died for the Republic. My daddy blinked his eyes when he heard this, and he got up and went into the yard for a long time.

The next day was the funeral. Black shiny horses with their mouths all suds, and silver buckles on their straps, came trotting into the street. All the wee lads were looking at themselves in the glossy backs of the cabs where you could see yourself all fat and funny like a dwarf. I didn't play, because Johnny was dead and I had on a new, dark suit. Jack Byrne was out playing and he told me that we had only two cabs and that there were three cabs at his daddy's funeral. There were crowds of peelers in the street, some of them talking to tall, red-faced men with overcoats and walking sticks.

Three men along with my daddy carried the yellow coffin down the stairs. There was a green, white and gold flag over it. But a thin policeman, with a black walking stick and black leggings, pulled the flag off the coffin when it went into the street. Then a girl snatched the flag out of the peeler's hands and he turned all pale. At the end of our street there were more peelers and every one wore a harp with a crown on his cap. Brother Gabriel used to fairly wallop us in school if we drew harps with crowns on them. One day we told him the peelers wore them on their caps. 'Huh!' he said. 'The police! the police! They don't love their country. They serve England. England, my boys! The England that chased our people to live in the damp bogs! The England that starved our ancestors till they had to eat grass and nettles by the roadside. And our poor priests had to say Mass[9] out on the cold mountains! No, my dear boys, never draw a harp with a crown on it!' And then he got us to write in our books:

Next to God I love thee
Dear Ireland, my native land!

'It's a glorious thing,' he said, 'to die for Ireland, to die for Ireland!' His voice got very shaky when he said this and he turned his back and looked into the press. But Brother Gabriel is not in the school now; if he was he'd be good to me, because our Johnny died for Ireland.

The road to the cemetery was lined with people. Little boys that were at my school lifted a fringe of hair when the coffin passed. The trams were stopped in a big, long line – it was nice to see so many at one look. Outside the gates of the graveyard there was an armoured car with no one peeping his head out. Inside it was very still and warm with the sun shining. With my daddy I walked behind the carried coffin and it smelt like the new seats in the chapel. The crowds of people were quiet. You could hear the cinders on the path

[9] Catholic name for the Communion service

squanching as we walked over them, and now and again the horses snorting.

I began to cry when I saw the deep hole in the ground and the big castles of red clay at the side of it. A priest, with a purple sash round his neck, shovelled a taste of clay on the coffin and it made a hard rattle that made me cry sore. Daddy had his head bowed and there were tears in his eyes, but they didn't run down his cheeks like mine did. The priest began to pray, and I knew I'd never see Johnny again, never, never, until I'd die and go to heaven if I kept good and didn't say bad words and obeyed my mammie and my daddy. But I wouldn't like Daddy to tell me to give away the pigeons. When the prayers were over a tall man with no hat and a wee moustache stood beside the grave and began to talk. He talked about our Johnny being a soldier of the Republic, and, now and then, he pointed with his finger at the grave. As soon as he stopped talking we said the rosary and all the people went away. I got a ride back in a black cab with my daddy and Uncle Pat and Uncle Joe. We stopped at the Bee Hive and they bought lemonade for me and porter for the cab driver. And then we went home.

I still have the pigeons and big Tom Duffy helps me to clean the shed and let them out to fly. Near night I give them plenty of corn so that they'll sleep long and not waken Daddy in the morning. When I see them fattening their necks and cooing I clod them off the slates.

Yesterday I was lying on the waste ground watching the pigeons and Daddy came walking towards me smoking his pipe with the tin lid. I tried to show him the pigeons flying through the clouds. He only looked at them for a minute and turned away without speaking, and now I'm hoping he won't wring their necks.

The Fly

by Katherine Mansfield

The First World War, also known as the Great War, lasted for four years. It destroyed lives on a scale previously unknown: the military figure of known deaths is 8.5 million, with 21 million injured, but it is estimated that over 10 million were killed. The assassination of Archduke Francis Ferdinand in Sarajevo on 28 June 1914, by Serb nationalist supporters, was the spark that ignited the war. The Archduke was heir to the throne of Austria-Hungary. That country declared war on Serbia exactly one month later. Russia supported Serbia and began to mobilise its troops. Germany, as a result of a pact with Austria-Hungary, mobilised its troops against Serbia. War then became inevitable. Germany declared war on Russia on 1 August, and on the 3rd declared war against France. It was when Germany invaded Belgium, ignoring a warning from Britain, that Britain declared war on Germany (4 August).

Britain believed the war would last only until Christmas. There was no conscription in Britain at the beginning of the war; 2 million volunteered to fight for their country. By 1916, it was becoming obvious that the expected victory was not coming as soon as hoped. Conscription for military service was introduced in that year, meaning that if you were old enough you had to fight. Katherine Mansfield's brother, Leslie Beauchamp, was killed in the war in 1915.

'Y'are very snug in here,' piped old Mr Woodifield, and he peered out of the great, green-leather armchair by his friend the boss's desk as a baby peers out of its pram. His talk was over; it was time for him to be off. But he did not want to go. Since he had retired, since his ... stroke, the wife and the girls kept him boxed up in the house every day of the week except Tuesday. On Tuesday he was dressed and brushed and allowed to cut back to the City for the day. Though what he did there the wife and girls couldn't imagine. Made a nuisance of himself to his friends, they supposed ... Well, perhaps so. All the same, we cling to our last pleasures as the tree clings to its last leaves. So there sat old Woodifield, smoking a cigar and staring almost greedily at the boss, who rolled in his office chair, stout, rosy, five years older than he, and still going strong, still at the helm. It did one good to see him.

Wistfully, admiringly, the old voice added, 'It's snug in here, upon my word!'

'Yes, it's comfortable enough,' agreed the boss, and he flipped the *Financial Times* with a paper-knife. As a matter of fact he was proud of his room; he liked to have it admired, especially by old Woodifield. It gave him a feeling of deep, solid satisfaction to be planted there in the midst of it in full view of that frail old figure in the muffler.[1]

'I've had it done up lately,' he explained, as he had explained for the past – how many? – weeks. 'New carpet,' and he pointed to the bright red carpet with a pattern of large white rings. 'New furniture,' and he nodded towards the massive bookcase and the table with legs like twisted treacle. 'Electric heating!' He waved almost exultantly[2] towards the five transparent, pearly sausages glowing so softly in the tilted copper pan.

[1] scarf
[2] triumphantly joyful

But he did not draw old Woodifield's attention to the photograph over the table of a grave-looking boy in uniform standing in one of those spectral photographers' parks with photographers' storm-clouds behind him. It was not new. It had been there for over six years.

'There was something I wanted to tell you,' said old Woodifield, and his eyes grew dim remembering. 'Now what was it? I had it in my mind when I started out this morning.' His hands began to tremble, and patches of red showed above his beard.

Poor old chap, he's on his last pins,[3] thought the boss. And feeling kindly, he winked at the old man, and said jokingly, 'I tell you what. I've got a little drop of something here that'll do you good before you go out into the cold again. It's beautiful stuff. It wouldn't hurt a child.' He took a key off his watch-chain, unlocked a cupbroad below his desk, and drew forth a dark, squat bottle. 'That's the medicine,' said he. 'And the man from whom I got it told me on the strict Q.T.[4] it came from the cellars at Windsor Castle.'

Old Woodifield's mouth fell open at the sight. He couldn't have looked more surprised if the boss had produced a rabbit.

'It's whisky, ain't it?' he piped feebly.

The boss turned the bottle and lovingly showed him the label. Whisky it was.

'D'you know,' said he, peering up at the boss wonderingly, 'they won't let me touch it at home.' And he looked as though he was going to cry.

'Ah, that's where we know a bit more than the ladies,' cried the boss, swooping across for two tumblers that stood on the table with the water-bottle, and pouring a

[3] legs
[4] in complete secrecy – Q.T. stands for 'quiet'

generous finger into each. 'Drink it down. It'll do you good. And don't put any water with it. It's sacrilege[5] to tamper with stuff like this. Ah!' He tossed off his, pulled out his handkerchief, hastily wiped his moustaches, and cocked an eye at old Woodifield, who was rolling his in his chaps.[6]

The old man swallowed, was silent a moment, and then said faintly, 'It's nutty!'

But it warmed him; it crept into his chill old brain – he remembered.

'That was it,' he said, heaving himself out of his chair. 'I thought you'd like to know. The girls were in Belgium last week having a look at poor Reggie's grave, and they happened to come across your boy's. They're quite near each other, it seems.'

Old Woodifield paused, but the boss made no reply. Only a quiver in his eyelids showed that he heard.

'The girls were delighted with the way the place is kept,' piped the old voice. 'Beautifully looked after. Couldn't be better if they were at home. You've not been across, have yer?'

'No, no!' For various reasons the boss had not been across.

'There's miles of it,' quavered old Woodifield, 'and it's all as neat as a garden. Flowers growing on all the graves. Nice broad paths.' It was plain from his voice how much he liked a nice broad path.

The pause came again. Then the old man brightened wonderfully.

'D'you know what the hotel made the girls pay for a pot of jam?' he piped. 'Ten francs! Robbery, I call it. It was a little pot, so Gertrude says, no bigger than a half-

[5] misuse of something sacred
[6] mouth

crown. And she hadn't taken more than a spoonful when they charged her ten francs. Gertrude brought the pot away with her to teach 'em a lesson. Quite right, too; it's trading on our feelings. They think because we're over there having a look round we're ready to pay anything. That's what it is.' And he turned towards the door.

'Quite right, quite right!' cried the boss, though what was quite right he hadn't the least idea. He came round by his desk, followed the shuffling footsteps to the door, and saw the old fellow out. Woodifield was gone.

For a long moment the boss stayed, staring at nothing, while the grey-haired office messenger, watching him, dodged in and out of his cubby-hole like a dog that expects to be taken for a run. Then: 'I'll see nobody for half an hour, Macey,' said the boss. 'Understand? Nobody at all.'

'Very good, sir.'

The door shut, the firm heavy steps recrossed the bright carpet, the fat body plumped down in the spring chair, and leaning forward, the boss covered his face with his hands. He wanted, he intended, he had arranged to weep . . .

It had been a terrible shock to him when old Woodifield sprang that remark upon him about the boy's grave. It was exactly as though the earth had opened and he had seen the boy lying there with Woodifield's girls staring down at him. For it was strange. Although over six years had passed away, the boss never thought of the boy except as lying unchanged, unblemished in his uniform, asleep for ever. 'My son!' groaned the boss. But no tears came yet. In the past, in the first months and even years after the boy's death, he had only to say those words to be overcome by such grief that nothing short of a violent fit of weeping could relieve him. Time, he had declared then, he had told everybody, could make no difference. Other men perhaps might recover, might live their loss down, but not he. How was it possible? His boy was an only son. Ever since his birth the boss had worked at building up this business for him; it had no other meaning if it was not for the boy. Life itself had come to have no other meaning. How on earth could he have slaved, denied himself, kept going all those years without the promise for ever before him of the boy's stepping into his shoes and carrying on where he left off?

And that promise had been so near being fulfilled. The boy had been in the office learning the ropes for a year before the war. Every morning they had started off together; they had come back by the same train. And what congratulations he had received as the boy's father! No wonder; he had taken to it marvellously. As to his popularity with the staff, every man jack of them down to old Macey couldn't make enough of the boy. And he wasn't in the least spoilt. No, he was just his bright natural self, with the right word for everybody, with that boyish look and his habit of saying, 'Simply splendid!'

But all that was over and done with as though it never had been. The day had come when Macey had handed him the telegram that brought the whole place crashing about his head. 'Deeply regret to inform you ...' And he had left the office a broken man, with his life in ruins.

Six years ago, six years ... How quickly time passed! It might have happened yesterday. The boss took his hands from his face; he was puzzled. Something seemed to be wrong with him. He wasn't feeling as he wanted to feel. He decided to get up and have a look at the boy's photograph. But it wasn't a favourite photograph of his; the expression was unnatural. It was cold, even stern-looking. The boy had never looked like that.

At that moment the boss noticed that a fly had fallen into his broad inkpot, and was trying feebly but desperately to clamber out again. Help! Help! said those struggling legs. But the sides of the inkpot were wet and slippery; it fell back again and began to swim. The boss took up a pen, picked the fly out of the ink, and shook it on to a piece of blotting-paper. For a fraction of a second it lay still on the dark patch that oozed round it. Then the front legs waved, took hold, and, pulling its small, sodden body up, it began the immense task of cleaning the ink from its wings. Over and under, over and under, went a leg along a wing as the stone goes over and under the scythe.[7] Then there was a pause, while the fly, seeming to stand on the tips of its toes, tried to expand first one wing and then the other. It succeeded at last, and, sitting down, it began, like a minute cat, to clean its face. Now one could imagine that the little front legs rubbed against each other lightly, joyfully. The horrible danger was over; it had escaped; it was ready for life again.

But just then the boss had an idea. He plunged his pen back into the ink, leaned his thick wrist on the blotting-paper, and as the fly tried its wings down came a great heavy blot. What would it make of that? What indeed! The little beggar seemed absolutely cowed,[8] stunned, and afraid to move because of what would happen next. But then, as if painfully, it dragged itself forward. The front legs waved, caught hold, and, more slowly this time, the task began from the beginning.

[7] long-handled tool with a curved blade, used for cutting grass; the blade was sharpened with a stone
[8] overawed with fear

He's a plucky little devil, thought the boss, and he felt a real admiration for the fly's courage. That was the way to tackle things; that was the right spirit. Never say die; it was only a question of ... But the fly had again finished its laborious task, and the boss had just time to refill his pen, to shake fair and square on the new-cleaned body yet another dark drop. What about it this time? A painful moment of suspense followed. But behold, the front legs were again waving; the boss felt a rush of relief. He leaned over the fly and said to it tenderly, 'You artful little b ...' And he actually had the brilliant notion of breathing on it to help the drying process. All the same, there was something timid and weak about its efforts now, and the boss decided that this time should be the last, as he dipped the pen deep into the inkpot.

It was. The last blot fell on the soaked blotting-paper, and the draggled fly lay in it and did not stir. The back legs were stuck to the body; the front legs were not to be seen.

'Come on,' said the boss. 'Look sharp!' And he stirred it with his pen – in vain. Nothing happened or was likely to happen. The fly was dead.

The boss lifted the corpse on the end of the paper-knife and flung it into the waste-paper basket. But such a grinding feeling of wretchedness seized him that he felt positively frightened. He started forward and pressed the bell for Macey.

'Bring me some fresh blotting-paper,' he said sternly, 'and look sharp about it.' And while the old dog padded away he fell to wondering what it was he had been thinking about before. What was it? It was ... He took out his handkerchief and passed it inside his collar. For the life of him he could not remember.

The Deserter

by Ralph Elwell-Sutton

They brought him in the night I was on guard. They brought him into the guardroom around about one o'clock, when I was trying to sleep before my second shift. He was long-haired and unshaven, but I could not see much of the way he looked by the light of the single oil-lamp in the guardroom. He simply stood there in silence in an attitude of utter weariness, while the guard commander took down particulars for his report.

He had deserted[1] the day war broke out. He hadn't turned up with the rest of his Territorial unit, and the police had been looking for him pretty well ever since. Finally they had traced him, and they had brought him in that night I was on guard. That was about eleven weeks after the beginning of the war.

It was bound to be a court-martial[2] case, of course. We all knew it was bound to be a court-martial case, but we reckoned it wouldn't be so bad. The old-timers gave him a couple of months CB, all found. It wouldn't be a prison case. Some of us wondered if it wouldn't be better for the poor devil if they did make it a prison case. Maybe that was what he was hoping for, they said, so he wouldn't have to go to the war.

They didn't court-martial at once. For the time being they made him a regular mess-orderly in the men's

[1] abandoned the army without intending to return
[2] court for trying military or naval offences

mess,[3] and confined him to barracks. This would go on until the court martial, they told him; but they could not say how soon that would be.

So he was there in the mess the next day. He was shaven now, but his hair was still uncut, and he was still dark around the chin, He was the sort of chap who would never look shaven, however close he had shaved. He was very dark altogether, and his eyes were dark too. They were big eyes, dumb, and I suppose you might have said like a dog's, though I would have shuddered to see a dog with those eyes. Every now and then some of the men stopped to talk to him and ask him how it was going, and he would grin back at them slowly, and not say very much. He didn't say very much ever, but just grinned in that slow way of his, whenever anyone stopped to talk to him. He went about his work in the mess slowly but methodically, He did not in any way try to arouse sympathy, by his look or the way he went about his work, but most of the men were sorry for him. I reckoned he was past caring about sympathy.

For a few days people talked about him from time to time. Someone said once: 'It's a bloody shame. They shouldn't let a chap like that into the Army. Plumb scared of war, that's his trouble. It's a bloody shame keeping a chap like that in the Army.'

'Why in hell did he join the Army?' someone else asked.

'His girl wanted him to.'

'Oh, hell.'

Then we talked about him being plumb scared of war. We were all plumb scared of war, we reckoned. But it seemed to be different with this chap. He couldn't stand anything to do with war. He couldn't stand all the

[3] where the ordinary soldiers eat in a group

men in uniform and the routine and the rifles. It killed him inside and he went about in misery and awful fear. Everything he saw and smelt and heard made it worse, and some of us began to wonder if it would slowly drive him mad.

He stuck it for ten days. For ten days he went around the tables serving out tea, and standing around in the mess, generally unshaven, and always untidy, until he became a part of the place, as much a part of it as the tables and the benches and the smell of stale food. He hadn't any friends, but everyone was decent with him, and he seemed to be getting along. Anyone who didn't feel sympathetic left him alone. You couldn't make jokes at him. You wouldn't have got anything out of it.

But I doubt if any of us realised how unhappy a life it was for him. We did not know the sort of chap he was, and at best that mess was a godless place. The unit was in improvised quarters at the time, and the men's mess was in the disused part of a cotton-mill. It was a grey shabby building, square as a prison, but neglected and decaying too, and you felt cold looking at it. It was the same inside. I have never known anything so wrapped in gloom as that empty ill-lit machine room, where the mess-tables were laid out. The white-washed walls were cracked and grey now and came away in flakes, if you brushed past, and made you cough. The damp ceiling hung with ancient cobwebs, and only a sickly wan[4] light found its way through the small dust-caked windows. Here and there would be a pane missing, but it was not enough to make any difference. Some of the space was taken up with pieces of broken twisted machinery, flung together and rusting, like the wreckage of a bombed town. It was all right, of course, when the men

[4] pale and weak looking

were there, packed together, banging the tables and yelling for the orderlies and across at each other to make themselves heard: though even then there were men who would confide in you that the place got under their flesh.

The deserter was here nearly all the day. After the men had gone, he would be there still, in the empty gloom, going around the tables, collecting basins and bread-baskets and sweeping up the refuse and slops over the rough damp floor. Four times during the ten days that he stuck it the electricity plant failed, so that in the evenings he had not even the comfort of the few electric bulbs hung from the steel girders that spanned the machine-room. Instead they brought up oil-lamps, which made awful flickering shadows in the corners of the room, and turned the pieces of twisted machinery into fantastic surrealist[5] shapes.

Even when his work was over, there was no escape from the mill. Between six o'clock and tattoo[6] at ten-thirty he had to report every half-hour in the guard-room. There was no escape for him. His work might be over by half-past eight, but there was no relief. He could not go out like the other chaps and sit over a pint of beer in the comfort of a warm taproom. There was no sense in it, if you had to be up and out every half-hour to go to the guardroom.

So he stuck it for ten days. On the eleventh day he deserted again, Someone saw him go out after he had finished work in the evening, and then he failed to report to the guard when his half-hour was up.

Over a week went by and he was still missing. When we talked about him, it generally finished with someone

[5] dream-like, distorted
[6] a signal made in the evening for soldiers to return to their quarters

looking at the ground or not quite at you and saying they'd find him in the river one day soon. I remember one of the chaps saying one day, as we were driving up in a lorry to the field, where we paraded: 'Ay, he were a queer chap. I reckon he's done himself in all right. He were just the kind of chap to do himself in. Queer bloke. There's something wrong with a chap, what gets like that.'

'Ought never to 've been in the mucking Army,' someone else said.

I didn't join in the talk this time, but listened in the dimness of the lorry.

'Nuts from the start, 'e were.'

'Bloody queer way 'e 'ad of looking at you.'

'Remember 'ow 'e used to stand around up in the mess there? Not looking at bloody anything. Oh Christ. Gave me the bloody creeps.'

'Only one thing to it, though. He was plumb scared of war. Come to that, so am I.'

'Who the bloody hell isn't?'

Then we reached the parade ground.

I suppose it might have been a week later, when I was on guard-duty again. I had a stripe now, so I was junior NCO[7] of the guard and did not actually mount guard myself. In the corner of the guardroom lay a brown suitcase and a pile of blankets and a palliasse. The corporal of the Regimental Police, who was on duty during the day and came off when the guard mounted for the night, came into the guardroom. He was an aggressive kind of chap. I didn't like him much. Nobody liked him much, but an RP has to face that. Nobody forced him to be an RP, anyway. He jerked his head towards the suitcase and the bedding.

[7] non-commissioned officer

'For Christ's sake nobody touch them things,' he said. 'Let 'em alone, see? Them's the deserter's. They not got to be touched.'

Corporal Hanley, who was guard commander, looked up from going through the late-pass lists and report sheets.

'Don't tell me they're bringing that bastard in again tonight,' he said.

They got a line on him,' said the RP.

'Just my luck, if they brought him in tonight.'

'Police know where he is,' said the RP. 'But I reckon you're safe tonight. Only don't nobody touch them things.'

'That's all right.'

'Do they reckon he's alive?' I asked.

'Couldn't say. If you ask me, I reckon they ought to drag the mucking river.'

The RP lowered himself on to a bench. I could see he was going to talk.

'Proper bastard, he were,' he began. 'Real proper bastard. We been through his stuff there. Been advertising in the mucking papers, he had. Said he was lonely. You know. Lonely 'eart seeks friend. Cor blimey. Proper soft bloody bastard.'

He paused. Corporal Hanley nodded, busy writing.

'You'd only got to look at him,' he said. 'Hey, what's the name of that mucker out there on guard now? I got to fill in this report.'

One of the other members of the guard went over and spelt him out the name. The RP went on: 'I'll let you have a look,' he said, speaking to Corporal Hanley. 'He was a queer bloody bastard all right. You can have a look, too,' he said to me.

He went over and fetched the case and slumped it down on the table.

'Orl right, orl right,' he ordered. 'Can't have everybody mucking around. You other bastards muck off. This ain't a bloody sewing party.'

He opened the case and took out a bundle of papers and drew a letter from the bundle.

'Here, look at this,' he said, handing it to me.

'What is it?'

'Answer to his bloody advert. Some kind of a tart he got hold of. Rare bloody couple they must've been.'

I took the letter and read it. It was a rotten thing to read the chap's letters, but I wanted to read it. I wasn't going to snigger over it, anyway.

It was quite a short letter, written in a very neat, copperplate hand, dated about eight months back. The girl wrote that she was lonely, too, and described herself a little, not her looks so much as the sort of girl she was, and ended with rather pathetic formality, saying she hoped this might be the beginning of a happy friendship. It wasn't a funny letter. It was tragic, not funny at all.

'Want to keep her address?' asked the RP.

I grinned at him.

'No, you keep it for yourself,' I said. 'I'm off women.'

'You got the right angle,' said the RP. 'You mark my words. That's where this mucker went wrong. Women. If he'd 'ave laid off women. He'd 've been sweet and pretty. He'd be sitting here the same as you and me, and nobody'd 've known the difference. Here's the advert he had put in the paper, what started all the shemozzle.'[8]

I could not help smiling at the notice he had sent in to the local paper. 'Young man (rejected lover) ...', it began. I could not help smiling at the style and that

[8] problems

tense novelettish cliché,[9] although I guessed it was sincere.

Along with the notice to the paper he had sent a long letter, in which he had poured out his soul. He wanted them to believe he was sincere and that his notice was not a joke. In an even, undeveloped round hand, absurdly unsuited to the passionate words it formed, he had bared his soul before them. There were four good-sized pages of it, and there was not a single mistake of grammar or spelling. I reckoned he had been hours over it. At the end he asked if they would please let him have an answer to the letter, even if it were only acknowledgement. He sent money for the notice to be inserted three times.

It was the hell of a letter. You did not need his protestations of sincerity. No man, who had not been nearly mad with loneliness, could have written it. With all its clichés and the absurd sedate handwriting, you had set out for you in that letter, naked and unvarnished, the awful tragedy of loneliness.

I handed the letter back to the RP.

'Let the Corporal have a dekko,'[10] he said.

Corporal Hanley ran his eye over it.

'Oh, God, I can't read this,' he said.

The RP took it and put it back with the rest of the papers in the case, and then shut the case and put it over in the corner again.

'Now don't let nobody touch that, or there'll be hell to pay,' he warned. He looked at his watch. 'Christ, I'm going to be late for my date. Good-night, you muckers,'

'Good-night, mucker.'

It was bloody cold in the guardroom that night.

[9] stale, over-used phrase typical of a sentimental short novel
[10] slang for 'have a look'

There was a howling wind outside, and the rain came in under the door and made a great pool in the middle of the guardroom floor. The tank and wick were missing from the oil-stove, and we had no heating. We played a few rounds of pontoon, but nobody seemed to want to play, and we didn't talk much. I think most of us had the deserter on our minds. In the lulls, when the wind dropped for a few seconds, we could hear the river roaring under the bridge and past the mill. I wondered what kind of a girl she had been, the one that answered his notice. I wondered if they had made out all right together, and I sort of thought it wouldn't be so bad, if they had been happy and stopped being lonely. I guessed it had been all right, when he first joined his unit in peacetime. She would never have wanted him to join, if she had known war was coming. Whichever way you looked at it, it was the war breaking out that had smashed everything. I remember him standing around in the mess, and his dark melancholy eyes, and the way he looked at nothing and then grinned slowly, when you spoke to him. I wondered why some people seemed to be predestined for tragedy, so that whatever happened it always ended in tragedy. I hoped very much that he had known for those last few months what it was like to be happy instead of tragic. I suppose I thought about it for hours. It was as cold and wild a night as I ever remember, and I kept my greatcoat on all the time.

I know that, as far as I was concerned, the tragedy was played that night. Three nights later, when I heard they had dragged him from the river some sixty miles away in a town I had never heard of, it did not mean anything to me at all.

Activities

DURING WAR AND DESTRUCTION

On the Quai at Smyrna (United States)

1. The tone of this story by Ernest Hemingway seems cold and detached as though the main character is not upset by the screaming at midnight he hears or the things he sees. Discuss what you think this tells us about the effect of war upon these men. Do they care? Have they heard so many screams and seen so many upsetting things that they don't feel anything any more?

2. Write a paragraph about what you think this story is telling us about war. Think about the main character: why might he be so detached? What could Hemingway be telling us about war through the reactions of this soldier?

3. Read the last sentence of this story again: 'My word yes a most pleasant business.' Debate in a group why this sentence comes as a surprise, remembering to focus on particular words to substantiate your points.

4. Imagine that you are the main character in this story. Write a letter to your commander back home describing the situation as clearly as you can. Remember that you have to write the truth but also that you must not let the commander think that you are unhappy in any way. Start the letter:

   Dear sir,
   This is _____ reporting . . .

5 Look at the last paragraph, which begins: 'The Greeks were nice chaps too.' Compare the meaning of 'nice' with the way the Greeks treated their animals. How can you tell that 'nice' is meant ironically?

6 From this story, write what you think Hemingway's attitude to war is. Consider how you feel this attitude has influenced his writing. How does Hemingway see war? What effects does it have upon people?

7 Compare *On the Quai at Smyrna* to *The Alien Skull*. In what ways do you feel the narrator and Private Mulhall are similar in their attitudes to their surroundings? In what ways are they also different?

A Certain Death (Nigeria)

1 All of the stories in this anthology are about war. Considering this, what are your predictions from Flora Nwapa's title: *A Certain Death*? Predict whose death it will be and why it occurs. Think what is 'certain' about it.

2 The saying 'There is no smoke without fire' means that when a person is accused of something, even if they are innocent, there must be a reason for why they have been accused; they must somehow deserve what is happening to them. It negates any idea that a mistake may have been made and suggests that everything happens for a reason. Try and relate this saying to the fact that the people believe the narrator's brother is evil because he has lost both his wife and child. Why do you think the people have reacted in this way? Discuss your ideas.

3. Conscription is the opposite of volunteering to go into the army. Conscription means that you have to go, it is your duty and you have no choice. Write a paragraph answer to the question: Why is conscription necessary, particularly in times of war?

4. Design a poster inviting men to join the army. Try to make the army sound exciting and masculine. Death does not persuade but honour and a sense of duty do.

5. Write a continuation of this story, starting with the fact that the narrator learns of the boy's death. Describe how she fears for her brother's life. Remember that there is a warning at the end of the story: 'This is the last warning. On Afo day, you must present the men for the army. If you don't your village head will be handed over to the army. Don't say you were not warned.' Aim to write one side of A4.

6. This story is written from a woman's perspective. We often associate war with men and a great many stories about war are written by men. What do we learn of the woman's experience of war from this story? In what ways can staying at home be as difficult to cope with as leaving and fighting in the war?

7. *A Certain Death* is written by a woman author. Select two stories from this anthology, written by men, and compare them to Flora Nwapa's story. From this comparison, what judgements can you make on the difference between a woman's and a man's perspective on war?

They Came (Britain)

1. In this story by Alun Lewis the soldier is called simply 'the soldier', 'he', 'the Welsh boy' or 'Taffy' – a nickname for a Welshman. Discuss in pairs why the soldier is not given a name. What effect does this have?

   If you find this difficult substitute a name and see what difference is created. For example the first line: 'The evening was slowly curdling the sky as **Stephen** trudged the last mile along the lane leading from the station to the Hampshire village . . .'

2. Discuss what impression is created of this soldier in the first paragraph. Consider his appearance as well as his actions. From this is it possible to guess what experiences he has had? How old do you think he is? What do you think he was like before he became 'the soldier'?

3. Read what Taffy says on page 19 again: 'You always pay in this life.' The word 'pay' doesn't refer here to money but instead means that we can pay with pain and experience. We are left wondering what price the soldier has had to pay. Write a paragraph of the soldier's thoughts to be placed in between his statement and Fred's remark: 'Why don't you take the girl, Taffy?' Your paragraph should start: 'The soldier sat and thought . . .' Your aim is to make the soldier's feelings of sadness and loss clear.

4. When asked if he had a good leave the soldier repeatedly replies: 'Yes, thanks, except for raids.' To the sergeant of the guard he replies: 'Not bad, except for the raids. Raided us the first night I was home.' Write a poem of four verses to be read out loud. The poem should be entitled 'The Raids'. After each verse include the soldier's reply above as a chorus. If you have difficulty use the following as your first verse:

The soldier was exhausted;
Too tired for games and conversation.
When asked about his leave
He invariably replied:

'Not bad, except for the raids.
Raided us the first night I was home.'

5 Imagine that you are the soldier many years later. You are sitting in a comfortable lounge looking through some old photographs. You begin to think back to your days as a soldier, some memories are happy but most sadden you.

Write a monologue as the soldier to be spoken aloud while he is looking through the photographs. You should base much of this on the story *They Came* but should also use your imagination.

6 Turn to the paragraph on page 27 that begins: 'They came over about eight o'clock the first night' and read until you reach 'But they were only playing a game with me, see?' (page 29). Write a front-page newspaper article based on the events contained within these paragraphs. You will need to invent a title for the paper and a heading for the article. The name of the town is not mentioned in the story so you may have to invent this as well.

You need to consider the layout of this article carefully. Decide on how old your audience will be as this will affect how you write the story. Use short paragraphs to convey the factual information. Try and keep your writing concise and to the point. Include a quotation from a witness.

7 Compare the soldier's experiences in this story by Alun Lewis with the narrator's in *A Certain Death*. The soldier has been subjected to an appalling experience and the narrator in Flora Nwapa's story is frightened for her brother's life. What similarities can you find in the male and female experiences illustrated in these stories?

The Upturned Face (United States)

1. The sound of the picks digging the earth is described as a 'dull beat' on page 32 in Stephen Crane's story. This is contrasted to the 'swift snap of close bullets'. Consider the difference between these two noises and what each says of the activity. Discuss this with a partner.

2. Why is it most satisfactory to Timothy Lean that the private places earth on the corpse's feet first?

3. Imagine that you, like Lean, have been ordered to search a dead man's body for 'things'. Start by looking at the body, carefully trying to avoid looking at the face, to make this a more impersonal task. Describe what you see and how you feel before, during and after your search. You should aim to write a side of A4 paper.

4. This story involves much tension. We see the anxiety of the men who wish to bury their comrade but are all too aware of the threat of enemy bullets bearing down upon them. We also witness the individual tensions of Lean and the adjutant. Consider how different this story would have been if it was not set in wartime. The funeral would have been prepared, with time enough to get things right. Write this alternative story, using the same characters, where there is no tension of the kind demonstrated in the story and where the funeral, in contrast, is peaceful and calm. Go back to the original, if you get stuck, and for each step (digging the earth – searching the body – throwing the

body into the shallow grave) consider what the alternative would be if they were not under pressure.

5. In a pair, act out Lean and the adjutant meeting after two whole years apart. The war is over and they meet at an army social function. The atmosphere is jovial and one of celebration. When they meet their initial conversation reflects this until Lean breaks the news that the private, who was wounded when they were burying their comrade, has since died. This introduces a more sombre note and the pair begin to remember the burial in more detail. Both desperately want to express the horror of that moment but are frightened to dwell upon it too deeply. Your conversation should end with both about to express their personal horror when they are interrupted. This conversation should contain tension which you can build up not only in words but in body language and use of pause also. When they begin to remember the burial, the dialogue should contrast to their earlier easy conversation and should be stilted and awkward but, every so often, broken by an almost violent piece of description.

6. This story is mainly told in dialogue between characters. Without using speech, write as though you are an onlooker watching this scene and describe what you see. You should describe the appearance of the men, their movements, the setting around you and their actions. You may wish to be either an enemy soldier, transfixed by this unusual scene, or a private of the same army but too afraid to help.

7. Select two other stories from this anthology which you feel are similar. Comment in detail on the similarities you have found and conclude with what each story has to tell us about war in general.

Summer Flower (Japan)

1. This short story is about the atomic bomb landing on Hiroshima in 1945. Considering this fact, it is a surprise that the title of this story is *Summer Flower*. Discuss in groups what this title suggests to you and then why you feel Tamiki Hara has given his story this title.

2. Make a list of points which would help to explain why the narrator feels as though he is 'standing stage centre in a tragic play' (page 40). Why does it all feel unreal to him, like a nightmare?

3. Look at the following sentences again on pages 38 and 39: 'August 15 would be the first anniversary for the soul of my wife, but it was doubtful whether my native town would survive until then' and 'It was on the third day after my visit to the grave that the bomb was dropped.' Both sentences contrast the passing of the narrator's wife with the imminent bombing of the town. Create two such sentences of your own, which contrast personal feeling of grief and loss with public destruction.

4. You have been asked to make an announcement on the radio about the bomb. You have been told to speak the facts but not to panic those listening. You need to say what time the bomb was dropped, how many people are dead and approximately how many are injured. You must also provide information on where to go in order to receive emergency treatment. All of this must be covered in forty to fifty words as this is all the length you are allowed.

5. Imagine that you are the headteacher of a mixed comprehensive school in Japan which is situated near enough to Hiroshima for some of the pupils to have been killed as well as their relatives and friends. You are going to

give an assembly where you break the news of those who are lost and ask for thoughts to be with their families and also those who are injured. You should end the speech on an encouraging note so that the children realise how important it is to help each other and that things will get better. The speech should be from half to one side of A4 long.

6 You are the commander of an emergency task force that is being sent in to Hiroshima to clear out the dead and take the injured to safety. You have a precious slot of three minutes to tell your crew of twenty what the situation is, what to expect and what their task is. As time is short you need to present clear, factual information and cannot afford to describe the situation in too much detail. Write what you would say to the crew and then time it to last exactly three minutes.

7 Your name is Tamira Tanara and you have been badly injured in the explosion. Write a letter to your family who live in Tokyo telling them about your experiences. Remember that you will have been badly shaken by this experience and desperately want your family to understand the horror that you have experienced so that they can understand.

8 Tamiki Hara was a witness to the atomic bomb of 1945. Consider first how you can tell that this story has arisen out of personal experience. Select sentences which you feel indicate that this is based on a real event and explain your reasons clearly. Conclude with how you feel this incident has affected Hara's writing and why after this event he continued to write about the dropping of the Hiroshima bomb.

9 Compare Tamiki Hara's story with *Two Friends*. In *Summer Flower* the narrator begins with a visit to his wife's grave.

The two friends in Guy de Maupassant's story are fishing before they are killed. How do both authors use the contrast between normal activities and the unnatural deaths that follow? In both cases, what effect does war have upon their natural activities?

The Alien Skull (Ireland)

1. Mulhall, in Liam O'Flaherty's story written in 1924, doesn't touch the enemy soldier because he recognises the fact that the enemy is paralysed with fear (page 61) and that if he touched him he would struggle like a madman. Write a paragraph where Mulhall fails to recognise this and grasps the enemy by the throat.

2. Why has it become more difficult for Mulhall to remain brutal and calm, capturing the enemy and marching him back over the frosty ground? The enemy smiles and offers Mulhall bread. What vital ingredient of war has changed and why has it changed? Discuss this with a partner.

3. Imagine that you are making a film of this story. Decide who will play Mulhall and who the enemy. Neither has to be a well-known person; you can just describe what they would look like. Under the following headings, make at least five points in relation to each character: physical appearance, clothes, personality, movement, voice, home life, dreams and ambitions.

4. Consider a different ending to this story. Imagine that Mulhall was not killed and made it to his own line safely. When he returns, he is criticised for failing to bring back an enemy alive so he is sent out again. In journeying back, he has to pass the body of the man he killed. Write this

alternative ending. It is up to you whether or not Mulhall finds another enemy, if the same thing happens as with the first, or if he successfully captures him. Write at least two sides of A4 paper.

5 Many of you will be familiar with film trailers. Write the words to sell the film version of this story. Remember, you need to make it sound exciting and dramatic without giving too much of the plot away. Your trailer should be fifty words long. Practise reading it out and try different voices. If you are stuck, you could start: 'It was a time of war . . .'

6 Compare this story to *The Fly* by Katherine Mansfield. What do Mulhall and the boss have in common in their attitude to the enemy and the fly, respectively? What do these two stories tell us about war and the effects of it?

THE CONSEQUENCES AND EFFECTS OF WAR

The Making of Me (Britain)

1. Between Granda and the young boy there are two generation gaps. Discuss why it is that a generation gap of this kind can lead to a lack of communication. You should come up with a list of factors that would explain why this can happen. If you are stuck, consider the way in which society has changed: transport, medicine, science – and think about how changes such as these may affect relationships between generations. The boy even remarks that the birth of his father seemed as far off as the 'Pharaohs building the pyramids'.

2. Why is the boy so fascinated with his grandfather? Does it seem strange to you? Explain your reasons. Find five things that particularly interest the boy about Granda's appearance. To what extent do any of these suggest that he seems to be a monster in the eyes of his grandson?

3. The grandfather tries to drown the memories he never speaks of. Imagine that you are the grandfather and that you are troubled with nightmares where these memories plague you and come alive. Write in detail about what you see in these dreams. Try to make the horror of your past experiences come to life. Describe what you see, hear, smell, taste and feel. Remember that as it is a dream sequence the events do not have to come in any particular order but can overlap, almost as though there are so many memories that they all come crowding in at once.

4. The boy comments that he has learnt that every object tells a story. Imagine that you are the voice of an old, tarnished medal made from iron. On it are written the words 'For bravery in the Great War'. Write a paragraph of your story,

commenting on who you belonged to and where you have been.

5 Taking two lines, one to represent the grandfather and the other for the boy, plot a graph. When the two lines are furthest apart the communication between them is poor (the boy still considers Granda to be a monster). When the lines are closer to each other the two characters are becoming friends. When the lines meet, the two have become 'good chums'. Write next to the intersection at what point in the story this occurs.

Look at your graph. Are the lines far apart at the beginning and how long do they remain so? What actually brings them together – is there any one incident?

6 Many years later the boy has grown into a grandfather himself, with memories of his own. His grandson is sitting on his knee and they are looking at a photograph album. His grandson finds a picture of Granda and asks his grandfather to tell him a story about this strange-looking man. Write this story as a fairy story where Granda is at first an evil monster but by the end of the story discovered to be a kind man. Start your story with: 'Once upon a time . . .'

7 Contrast the boy's relationship with his grandfather in Robert Westall's story with Frankie's relationship with Johnny in *Pigeons*. In what ways are both the boy and Frankie fascinated by Granda and Johnny, respectively? How do these figures influence their younger counterparts?

The Coup de Grâce (United States)

1. Ambrose Bierce writes that the 'very taste of battle was in the air'. Consider how a person might be able to 'taste' battle. Discuss with a partner what elements you might be able to taste from a battle. Draw up a list of those elements so strong that they affect the sense of taste.

2. When the officer, Captain Madwell, finds a small group of bodies in a shallow ravine, one body moves. The author refers to this person as an 'it', which implies that the officer considers this person to be an object rather than a 'he'. Why do you think this is? What does this suggest?

3. Sergeant Caffal Halcrow and the horse are both injured. By their individual facial expressions, they make it clear that they need Madwell's help. In the sentence following his seeing the horse, Madwell shoots it, indicating that he is acting immediately. He is then able to find the courage to help his friend. Considering this, why do you think the author included the horse in his story? What does it add to the dramatic tension of the situation?

4. Imagine that Major Creede Halcrow, Caffal Halcrow's brother, misinterpreted Captain Madwell's action of mercy – the 'coup de grâce' – and informs the necessary officials. Working with a partner, imagine that both Madwell and Halcrow are ordered to appear in front of the military court. Decide who you want to play and each prepare a statement, of approximately seventy words, where you explain what happened in your opinion and sum up with your feelings about what took place.

5. Create a storyboard where you tell this story in six boxes, using both pictures and writing. Divide a piece of plain

paper into the boxes and allow a two-centimetre gap at the bottom of each box for writing.

6 Find the paragraph that begins 'There was no misreading that look' (page 84). From the sentence that opens 'Consciously or unconsciously' read until you reach '*coup de grâce*'. Look up the words that you do not understand, for example: 'boon', 'incarnate' and 'rite' and rewrite the extract in your own words.

7 If Captain Madwell had not killed Sergeant Caffal Halcrow, this story would have had a different ending. Caffal would have been taken off to military hospital and Madwell would have been left with feelings of guilt that he didn't help his friend. Imagine that the author decided to change the ending and did not include the last sentence: 'The third was Major Creede Halcrow.' Madwell is now unable to kill his friend after shooting the horse, the hospital attendants arrive and remove Caffal. Major Creede is left with Madwell, who is staring helplessly at the other bodies. Write this alternative ending, which should be at least one side of A4 paper long, and should cover both Madwell's and Creede's feelings, then describe what happens at the hospital.

8 Compare and contrast this story by Ambrose Bierce to *They Came*. Look at the two characters of Madwell in *The Coup de Grâce* and the soldier in Alun Lewis's story. Consider how both of these characters suffer because of the loss of a loved one. Compare and contrast their feelings to see what similarities and differences you can find.

Two Friends (France)

1. Discuss why the two men are 'intimidated by the silence all around them' on page 90. What are they afraid will happen? How can silence be intimidating? Imagine a situation where you are frightened and are surrounded by silence. Do your senses become more acute?

2. In a pair act out a Prussian officer questioning either Monsieur Sauvage or Monsieur Morissot on what they are doing there. The officer should be threatening and have an accusing tone. The Monsieur should reply truthfully and try to diffuse the situation.

3. Write a paragraph answer to the following questions:

   a) What is the choice that the two friends are given?

   b) Why is this choice so difficult?

4. Take the two words 'peace' and 'war' and draw spider diagrams for both. Write down all the words you associate with each word. For example, noise and conflict would go with *war*, whereas silence and friendship would relate to *peace*.

5. Write a paragraph, as if you were Morissot, explaining why man will never be free. All the help you need is in the text. You should sound factual but cynical also as though learning why man will never be free has cost you pain.

6. Consider how different this story would be if it ended before the Prussians came out and captured the two men. How differently would the reader feel at the end of each story?

7. Imagine that you are a newspaper reporter who has been asked to write a 500-word article about the murder of these

two men. You only know the bare facts: they had been fishing and were shot by Prussian soldiers. You are given clearance to interview the soldiers, who indicate in their replies to your questions that the Frenchmen were believed to be spies. You believe that they are not telling the truth but you need to quote them in your article. In your article include what little you know but also try to tell your readers about what you feel is the tragedy of this story: that two innocent men can have their peace so shatteringly destroyed.

8 In Guy de Maupassant's story, two Frenchmen are killed by Prussians when they are fishing. This gives a strong sense of irony to the ending of the story, where we see the German officer about to eat the fish that the two companions caught at the beginning. In *The Coup de Grâce* Madwell has to shoot his friend, Caffal Halcrow, in order to save him from a long, painful death. Look at the end of both these stories and compare the Prussian officer in *Two Friends* with Madwell in Ambrose Bierce's story. How differently do they behave and how differently do they look upon the shooting, if they think about it at all?

Pigeons (Ireland)

1 From your knowledge of Frankie's life with Johnny, in Michael McLaverty's story, act out an interview with Frankie where he reminisces about his life with Johnny. Remember that this should be full of pleasant memories. Then the interviewer questions Frankie about Johnny's death. All the pleasure and fond memories are now gone for Frankie and you should reflect this in his replies and tone of voice. Spend five minutes on each section and swap over roles with your partner.

2. Look at the paragraph that begins 'We were just ready . . .' on page 102 and select the details which you feel suggest that Johnny is not going to be all right.

3. Consider the remark that all the women who come to pay their last respects to Johnny make to Frankie's mother: 'I'm sorry for your trouble, but he died for his country.' The use of the word 'but' provides an exception, an explanation. Johnny is dead which is a sad thing *but* he died an honourable and unselfish death. Consider also Brother Gabriel's words: '"It's a glorious thing," he said, "to die for Ireland, to die for Ireland!"' ('Brother' means that he is a Catholic monk.) Design a poster encouraging and persuading potential soldiers that dying for one's country is an honourable thing. You can use any country.

4. At the funeral, when the prayers are over, 'a tall man with no hat and a wee moustache' begins to talk, declaring Johnny to be a 'soldier of the Republic' – meaning that his death was honourable because it was for his country. Imagine that you are this man and that instead of supporting Johnny's death you are against it and see it as a sign that the killing should stop. You feel his death was a waste. You must persuade those listening that it is time for peace. Write one side of A4.

5. The voice of Frankie is not a cynical or resigned one but it is more of a story-telling voice, as an onlooker to the happenings. This contrasts with the narrator in *Summer Flower* whose voice is resigned and who is more actively the witness to the destruction around him. Considering this contrast, select two passages from each story which you feel reflect this and explain why, in reference to the language.

The Fly (New Zealand)

1. Discuss why this story by Katherine Mansfield is called *The Fly* and not *The Son*. Why does the narrator forget his son when he experiments with the fly?

2. What is the boss trying to prove by playing with the fly? What is it that forces him to squirt the last drop of ink, knowing that the fly will die?

3. The boss received a telegram informing him of his son's death. Write the rest of the telegram from 'Deeply regret to inform you'. It must not be more than thirty words in length and needs to include details of how the son died and where his body is being kept. Remember that each word costs money and so you should aim to use as few as possible.

4. Imagine that you are the boss. Write two diary entries: one before the outbreak of war in 1914, when your son was working with you. Indicate how happy you are in this diary entry and that your son is settling into work well. You should also reflect on your future plans for him. The second diary entry is written one week after you received news of your son's death. You should comment on your deep loss and anger that your boy has been taken so prematurely from you.

5. Imagine that you are the local Member of Parliament for this area. You hear of the boy's death and decide to use this in a speech against war in the House of Commons. This speech should be at least one side of A4 long and should describe the devastating effect that this loss has had on the boss. You want this personal account to upset people and make them want to end the war before their sons are taken from them also.

6 The fly struggles and struggles to live and be free of the ink. Imagine that the fly is a soldier and the ink symbolises the bullets coming from the enemy. Write your own story where the boss is the merciless enemy, directing rounds of bullets at you, and you are the soldier to be experimented upon. Provide detail and description of your fight and final collapse. Aim to write at least three sides of A4.

7 Contrast this story by Katherine Mansfield with *The Deserter*. In *The Fly*, we see a man who is both strong, in coming to terms with his son's death, and weak, by experimenting with a defenceless fly. Compare the strength and weakness of this man to those of the deserter in Ralph Elwell-Sutton's story. What similarities and differences can you find?

The Deserter (Britain)

1 Discuss why you feel some soldiers desert the army. Are they simply cowards? Should we give soldiers a choice whether they fight in a war or not?

2 Work in a pair with one of you being the deserter in the story, recently brought back against your free will, and the other a sergeant in command of the troops. Imagine that you are in a small room alone and that it is the sergeant's job to find out why the soldier deserted and also to tell him of his punishment.

3 You have been asked to write two or three paragraphs about desertion that will appear in a soldier's manual. You need to define what deserting means, why it happens and what the punishment is. At the end you should include a list of names of deserters and of the punishments they

received. Remember that the army is not in favour of desertion and so your paragraphs should contain an explicit warning.

4. Write the last page of the letter that the deserter sent to the newspaper. For help and ideas read the comments about the letter in the story.

5. Read through the following sentences again on page 117: 'Then we talked about him being plumb scared of war. We were all plumb scared of war, we reckoned. But it seemed to be different with this chap. He couldn't stand anything to do with war. He couldn't stand all the men in uniform and the routine and the rifles. It killed him inside and he went about in misery and awful fear.' Select the detail which shows that the deserter is scared of war. Write a diary entry, as though you are the deserter, where you reflect these fears and your feelings. Put yourself in his position and think about how he feels.

6. Consider why Ralph Elwell-Sutton chose to write about a deserter. What is he trying to tell us about some individuals' experience of war?

7. Imagine that you are the deserter in this story and that you witness the burial of the corpse in *The Upturned Face*. Think about what you know of the deserter and write a story of his reactions to witnessing this event, including his return to the guardroom and his inability to express his horror at seeing the earth cover the upturned face in Stephen Crane's story. You should aim to write two sides of A4 paper.

Coursework assignments

Creative

1. Imagine that you were responsible for putting together this collection of short stories about war. The series editor has told you that you need to write an introduction of 100 words, informing the reader what this anthology is aiming to do. If you are stuck, read the introduction at the beginning of this book but remember that yours must not be the same.

2. After reading these stories you should either feel inspired to write one of your own or have enough information to be able to write one successfully. Imagine that you have the opportunity to include a story about war in this anthology. Write your own of at least two sides of A4 in length. Remember to be original.

3. Write a collection of poems on war, designed to make people think carefully about what war means in real terms and to encourage them not to forget those who have already lost their lives.

Comparison

4. Select two stories from this anthology and compare what both tell us about war. Write an essay that examines the subject of each story and in your conclusion contrast and compare their comments on war and its consequences. You should comment upon the style and language of both stories.

5. Select two stories from different periods. Examine the language of both carefully and write an analysis where you contrast and compare what each says of war.

6. Look carefully at the stories *The Making of Me* by Robert Westall and *Pigeons* by Michael McLaverty. Both authors have written from the perspective of a child. What do we learn about the child's experience from these stories? How does war play a part in the life of a child? Write a comparative essay on these stories in answer to this question.

Media

7. You are a journalist and have a weekly review column in the newspaper. Your boss has asked you to read and review this anthology of short stories. You are allowed 400 words to do this, no more, and no less than 350. You should start by making a general comment about the range and purpose of the collection and then focus your comments on two or three stories. Conclude your review by giving the book a star rating.

Social and historical context

8. Select one of the pre-twentieth-century stories and compare it to a twentieth-century story. Examine the language and style of each with a view to concluding what differences can be found. What does each story reveal about the time in which it was written?

The authors

Ambrose Bierce (1842–1914?) was an American journalist and short-story writer. He fought in the American Civil War of 1861–5 (in the Federal government army) and reached the rank of major. Bierce was bitter as a result of his experiences in the war and became known as 'Bitter Bierce'. This disillusionment is reflected in his short stories about the Civil War. When the war ended he became a journalist. In 1872 he moved to England and lived and wrote there for four years. Bierce became more estranged from his family and friends, and during the Civil War in Mexico he disappeared. It is not known exactly how or when he died.

Stephen Crane (1871–1900) was born in Newark, New Jersey, the last of fourteen children. He moved to New York City, where he worked as a journalist for the *Tribune* and the *Herald* before starting on his first novel (published 1893). Two years later his novel *The Red Badge of Courage,* set during the American Civil War, and a book of poems made him internationally famous. In 1896 he published a collection of short stories, *The Little Regiment,* also focusing on the Civil War. The following year he travelled to Greece where he worked as a war correspondent. Poor health forced him to leave and he moved to England. He died from tuberculosis at the age of twenty-nine.

Ralph Elwell-Sutton (1913–?). *The Deserter* was printed in *Folios of New Writing* in the spring of 1940, published by the famous Hogarth Press which was founded by Leonard and Virginia Woolf. In the book it says of the author: 'After leaving Oxford he went into journalism and spent two years as a general reporter on a Kent newspaper. He gave this up to become a schoolmaster and learn Spanish. He joined the Signals Unit towards the end of last September.' He survived the war. His story was republished in *Penguin New Writing* in 1942. These books brought writing on war to the forefront: they were read by the fighting soldiers as well as by people at home.

Tamiki Hara (1905–51). Born in Hiroshima in Japan, Hara graduated from Keio University in English Literature. He published both short stories and poems in literary magazines but was not greatly acknowledged. After experiencing the atomic bomb in 1945 his writing style changed. *Summer Flower* was written two years later and describes the dreadful catastrophe that took place. He was awarded the Minakami Takitarō Prize for his work. Other work after this continued to be about the atomic bomb. He committed suicide.

Ernest Hemingway (1899–1961). Born in Chicago, the son of a keen sportsman, Hemingway spent a great deal of time at the Lakeside Hunting Lodge in Michigan which was to remain one of the most important landscapes for his imaginative writing. He became a reporter in 1917, worked as an ambulance driver on the Italian front, and covered the Graeco-Turkish war in 1922. In 1926 he established an international reputation with the novel *The Sun Also Rises*. He worked as a war correspondent in the Second World War. In 1954 he won the Nobel Prize, but his last years, spent in Cuba, were full of personal misfortune and he committed suicide.

Alun Lewis (1915–44) was born in South Wales. He joined the army in 1940 and went out to India. He used his experiences of war in his writing and published both poetry and short stories. His most acclaimed book of poetry is entitled *Raiders' Dawn*. It was the war that first led him to story-writing. He is quoted as having remarked that he saw war as 'providing the true story and the proper ending'. A lieutenant in a South Wales regiment, he was killed in an accident while on active service in Burma.

Michael McLaverty (1907–92) was born in Carrickmacross, in what is now the Republic of Ireland, and spent most of his life as a teacher and then headteacher in Belfast, in Northern Ireland. Highly regarded as a fiction writer in the 1930s, he enjoyed new popularity in the 1970s and 1980s, following the publication of his *Collected Short Stories*. His novel of 1939, *Call My Brother Back*, was reissued in 1989.

Katherine Mansfield (1888–1923). Born in Wellington, New Zealand, the daughter of an industrialist, she spent her early years in rural surroundings. This provided her with inspiration and is the background to many of her best short stories. She moved to England in 1903 and began to write short stories which, from 1918 onwards, were published in literary magazines. She always struggled to develop her skills, saying: 'I have a passion for technique.' She used small events to make deep points. To her despair, her brother was killed in a war accident in 1915. *The Fly* was one of her last stories and written when she knew that she was dying from tuberculosis.

Guy de Maupassant (1850–93) was born in Normandy, France, and stayed with his mother when his parents separated. When his first short story was published, entitled *Boule de Suif* (about the Franco-Prussian war), he left his job at the Civil Service and devoted himself to professional writing. He published numerous articles, about 300 short stories and six novels. In 1892, as a result of illness, he attempted suicide and was committed to a Paris asylum where he later died.

Flora Nwapa (Nwanzuruahal) (1931–   ) was born in East Nigeria and studied at Ibadan University College and Edinburgh University. She has taught and toured abroad, speaking on behalf of the Biafran cause during the Nigerian Civil War. She now runs a publishing house, Tana Press. Her first novel in 1966 established her as Nigeria's first woman novelist. *A Certain Death* appears in *Wives at War and Other Stories* (1980). She has also written for children.

Liam O'Flaherty (1897–1984) was born in the Aran Islands, off the west coast of Ireland. He studied at Dublin University, later returning to settle in Aran. He fought in the British Army during the First World War, and in Ireland fought on the side of the Republicans in the Civil War in the 1920s. He was a novelist as well as a short-story writer; his first novel, *The Neighbour's Wife*, was published in 1923. O'Flaherty won the Tait Memorial Prize for his third novel, *The Informer* (1926). *The Alien Skull* is from 1924.

Robert Westall (1929–93). Born in Tyneside, in north-east England, Westall grew up during the Second World War. He was educated in Fine Art and Sculpture, going on to teach art for twenty-five years. He published his first novel for children in 1975, entitled *The Machine Gunners*. It was an instant success and he was awarded the Carnegie Medal. Between 1985 and his death he retired to devote his time to writing.

Further reading

Poetry

The Collected Poems of Wilfred Owen edited by C. Day Lewis (Chatto & Windus, 1963)
Owen was born in Shropshire in 1893 and was killed in action in the First World War. He wrote poems based on his experiences of the war. Particularly moving are 'Dulce et Decorum Est' and 'Disabled'. The former deals with the irony between the conception that it is sweet and fitting to die for your country and the reality that it is painful and dirty. 'Disabled' is about a man who is left disabled after the war and who is plagued by memories of what he once was.

The Poetry of Protest edited by Simon Fuller (BBC/Longman, 1991)
Although not all of these poems have war as their subject, they are all a protest against unfavourable conditions, racism and conflict. You will be able to make comparisons between some of the issues raised in the short stories on war and these protest poems.

Short stories and novels

Echoes of War by Robert Westall (Puffin, 1989)
The story *The Making of Me* is contained in this anthology, along with four other stories whose subject is war. In each case Westall is drawing on his experiences of growing up through the war. It would be interesting to make a

comparison between one of these stories and *The Making of Me*.

The Mammoth Book of Modern War Stories edited by Jon E. Lewis (Robinson, 1993)
If you liked *On the Quai at Smyrna* by Ernest Hemingway then you can find another of his short stories contained in this anthology, *The Trick of El Sordo on the Hilltop*. Look out for Elizabeth Bowen's *Careless Talk* and an extract from Siegfried Sassoon's *Memoirs of an Infantry Officer*.

War of the Worlds by H. G. Wells (1898)
War machines arrive from Mars and devastate England. Panic spreads as London is destroyed. Survivors of the catastrophe live in hiding and dream of revolting against their new masters.

Women, Men and the Great War edited by Trudi Tate (Manchester University Press, 1995)
This is a very good collection of short stories about war and includes authors such as J. M. Barrie, Joseph Conrad, Katherine Mansfield and Virginia Woolf. Try *Gustav* by W. Somerset Maugham, which is about a spy in wartime.

Non-fiction

The Diary of Anne Frank by Anne Frank (Longman Imprint Books, 1989)
This is the diary of a young German Jewish girl during the Second World War. Her diary documents her family's remarkable existence, hidden from the Nazis in Amsterdam, and how they survived day to day until they were discovered and sent to concentration camps.

An Evil Cradling by Brian Keenan (Vintage, 1993)
Brian Keenan was born in Belfast in 1950 and after taking

degrees in English and Irish literature he went to Beirut University in Lebanon as a teacher. In 1985 he became international headline news when he was kidnapped by militiamen and held hostage for the next four and a half years. This book is Keenan's reflection and account of what he endured, in his personal war, during this time.

More Lives edited by Michael Simons and Barbara Bleiman (ILEA English Centre, 1987)
These six stories are written by school children and won the centre's 'Write '85' competition. These young authors write openly about death, war, escape and migration. Saroeun's story is about her family's escape from Cambodia and the pain and suffering they had to endure to flee the Khmer Rouge, the cruel rulers of the country.

Addison Wesley Longman Limited
Edinburgh Gate, Harlow,
Essex CM20 2JE, England
and Associated Companies throughout the world.

This educational edition first published 1997

Editorial material set in 10/12.5 pt Stone Sans
Produced by Longman Singapore Publishers (Pte) Ltd
Printed in Singapore

ISBN 0 582 28927 0

Cover photograph: Robert Harding Picture Library

The publisher's policy is to use paper manufactured from sustainable forests

Acknowledgements

We are grateful to the following copyright holders for permission to reproduce short stories:

African World Press Inc for 'A Certain Death' from *Wives at War and Other Stories* by Flora Nwapa. Copyright 1992. All rights reserved; Margaret Elwell-Sutton, executor to the estate of Ralph Elwell-Sutton , for 'The Deserter'; HarperCollins Publishers for 'They Came' from *The Last Inspection* by Alun Lewis (George Allen & Unwin, 1942); the Hemingway Foreign Rights Trust Manager for the short story 'On the Quai at Smyrna' from *The First Forty-Nine Stories* by Ernest Hemingway; Kodansha International Ltd for 'Summer Flower' by Tamiki Hara from *The Catch and Other War Stories*.. English translation copyright © 1981 by Kodansha International Ltd. All rights reserved; The Peters Fraser and Dunlop Group Ltd on behalf of the executor of the estate of Liam O'Flaherty for 'The Alien Skull' by Liam O'Flaherty from *Selected Short Stories* (Jonathan Cape) © Liam O'Flaherty 1937; Penguin Books Ltd for 'Two Friends' by Guy de Maupassant from *Selected Short Stories* by Guy de Maupassant, translated by Roger Colet (Penguin Classics, 1971) copyright © Roger Colet, 1971 & 'The Making of Me' by Robert Westall from *Echoes of War* by Robert Westall (Viking Kestrel, 1989) copyright © Robert Westall, 1989; Poolbeg Press Ltd for 'Pigeons' from *Collected Short Stories* by Michael McLaverty (1979).